Your beautiful soul,
like a warm hand to hold on a cold day
will continue to warm the lives you left behind.

Your laughter is in the Lock Haven mountains.
Your smile is in the endless stars on a warm summer night.
Your kind heart is among the spring flowers
and singing birds you loved so very much.

May your listening ear be wherever people need it.
May your compassion be carried on through those you loved.
May your kindness grow beyond all measure
from those who knew you well.

May peace come from understanding.

-Mama

His Beautiful Tortured Soul:

A look at the amazing, positive life
of a young man with bi-polar illness.

A tribute to my son John

By
C. Michelle Van Horn

For permission requests, write to the publisher, addressed "Attention: Permissions Coordinator," at the address below.

This work is a memoir and is my recollection of events along with a collection of journal entries and recollections of other contributors. I have aimed to portray them accurately and to the best of my knowledge. At no time are any entries intended to hurt or defame any parties mentioned but only to convey the story of John Van Horn.

ISBN-13: 978-1-7328407-0-6 (paperback)
LCCN: 2018911579

Inquires regarding His Beautiful, Tortured Soul should be directed via email to: hisbeautifultorturedsoul@gmail.com.com

Incredible front cover design by my nephew Adam Sheetz.
www.adamsheetzart.com

Book layout by Yana Boyd.
www.yanaboyd.com

First printing edition 2018.

1. Mental Illness—Bipolar Disorder
2. Child loss/Bereavement—Psychological aspects
3. Suicide
4. John Van Horn 1992-2015

Many thanks:

God in my life and faith in Jesus Christ

Mom: you have always been there, paid attention and knew enough to get me professional help during the rough times as a kid. You never threw in the towel.

Dad: I would have never gotten out without you.
I love you both!

My daughter Evelyn: You once told me I was your hero and it meant the world to me. You have inspired me far more than you will ever know. I love you Girmmy.

My Son Ethan: You have come farther than you realize. I know this book is difficult for you. You were such a huge part of John's world. Also, you were the "cutest baby". I love you.

Julia: My dearest friend. You have been so much to me, never judged, prayed unceasingly and I can't imagine surviving as long as I have without you. You stayed with John and me until the very end. Few friends would have done that. I will be forever grateful. I love you dear friend.

Erin: For being more than "okay" with this idea and sitting with me, sharing memories and stories, laughing and crying and adding so much to his story. Thank you above all, for loving John for who he was and always being there for him.

Brad: For your enthusiasm about this project, for being another set of eyes into his mind and for continuing to encourage him when you could have walked away.

Daniel and Patti

Too many others to name individually and I hope they understand

Table of Contents

Sufferings of the Mind

He who suffers not
understands not
the sufferings of the mind.
the torment within,
the depths of darkness
the cavernous pits of disconsolate despair.

The afflicted, full aware,
clashes with his own conflicted cerebrations
desperately attempting to overcome
the ever-absorbing abyss of blackness.
glimpsing, perhaps and attenuated coruscating beam
of promise upon which,
to anchor his last frantic grasp of hope.

Terribly short lived, the encouraging
turns immitigable, pointless.
The auspicious becomes the tragic.
He who suffers not
Understands not

Michelle Van Horn circa 2010

Preface

I think each day about John, my first born, and some thoughts are filled with painful heartache but more often than not they are joyful memories and good times. I see countless debates about mental health and "what should be done" and feel frustration but something that I find quite distressing is the misuse of mental health terms by people, especially young people, for ordinary quirky behavior in often times a humorous manner. You hear people make comments that they are OCD (obsessive compulsive disorder) because they like their bed made each morning. If people understood how difficult it is for a person who truly suffers with a severe case of OCD they may realize that they are just particular or neat. Hearing teens say they were in a bad mood in the morning and then felt happier that afternoon and say they must be bipolar or that a grumpy teacher is a bipolar bitch because they finally laid down the law with the class with a raised voice is unnerving. Comments such as this do little to increase proper awareness of mental health issues and makes it even less likely that sufferers will disclose their illnesses. They are actually very hurtful to those affected by, either personally or as one who cares about someone affected by any one of many mental illnesses.

Generally everything associated with mental health is negative. I'm not saying everyone should be going around wishing for a mental illness but with education people may not fear it. A condition such as Down's Syndrome, which used to be considered a horrible "birth defect", has organizations making huge strides in educating the public, medical community and political venues about this group and is changing the lives of these amazing people for the better. I dream of seeing things, such as this, happen for the mentally ill.

You are invited to step into the life an incredible young man. Meet him when he is born and watch him grow into the amazing young man he became. You will learn about his unstoppable musical talent and curiosity for the world. Discover his perseverance through trials, unending compassion for anyone and everyone and see him search for stability in his own mind. Cry with him as he fights for his sanity and question his abilities at every turn. Hear from his dedicated friends and family, and be astounded by the lives he touched by just being himself. Join John and those who traveled with him on a fantastic journey that will open your eyes to the amazing, positive life of a young man with bi-polar illness.

Introduction

My purpose for writing this book is first and foremost to honor the memory and extraordinary life of my son, John, who helped shape me into the person that I have become and continues to give me courage to push through bad days. I also hope to somehow inspire friends, families and offer people who come into contact with those who suffer with mental illness a better understanding of what life with mental illness is like on a daily basis. I truly hope that in my lifetime talking about, researching treatments for and helping those with mental illnesses will become as acceptable as cancer research and diabetes treatment.

I hope that people will no longer be afraid, ashamed or embarrassed to admit that they have a mental illness or that they need treatment. Far too many people do not seek treatment, stop treatment or refuse treatment because of the stigma attached to it. Our mental health system is failing us. I experienced it with my son and myself and have read many other accounts of it. It crosses all socioeconomic levels. (His Bright Light, Steel) You have to become your own, or loved one's advocate and hopefully never give up.

I wish for people to truly understand that living with and loving someone with a mental illness is not a hellish existence wrought with constant disaster and heartache. I have far more joyous memories with my son than sad. My heart broke for him and his struggles but that is what parents expect to do for average children too, but to a less intense degree. People with mental illnesses go through everyday trying to exist like everyone else; get up, go to school, hold a job, care for children, manage a home, vacation, relax, drive in traffic and juggle bills but, they force themselves to do it fighting their own mind and often in secret.

On bad days he and I would try to search for the best in it. Often we would conclude that if we lived in the dark ages we would have been put in an asylum and be in a cage so we were grateful for that. It's just how he was. We were positive for each other.

Where possible I have referenced other people's posted sentiments on John, personal journal entries in his own words and stories people were kind enough to relay. It is not my intention to speak ill of anyone through these descriptions but some stories have negative connotations that may help explain some of the developments in John's life. In the same way the positive stories also helped shape his beautiful soul as well. I hope the photographs help make him more real to you, help you see into his soul and connect with him, feel his music and hear his goofy laugh. I do wish for you to enjoy this journey. Although it has a sad ending it was a most spectacular life.

Quotes set apart throughout the text are posts, which appeared on Social Media at the time of John's passing. They have only been retyped for clarity rather than being scanned and to avoid posting photos of the authors.

My son's death certificate lists "cause of death" as suicide. Some days I accept that as truth, other days I do not. It's not because I am naive, but because I knew him like no one else and there is a lot more to it. How do I know this and how did he get to this end point? I will elaborate.

Michelle Sheetz Van Horn
August 4 at 6:00 am

It is with a broken heart and crushed spirit that I make this post. Yesterday, August 3, 2015, my first born, John Van Horn, died as a result of severe head trauma. I know he is with his Lord but it is no less painful to be without him. Those of you who knew John know that he touched every life he contacted. He will continue to do so as he will be able to donate a multitude of organs, many to children. I ask some things of you this day, pass this post on to those who knew him. Play a little loud music today to honor him, put on a band tee-shirt if you have one and remember a Johnny story if you have one. Think of his brother and sister too please. I have no idea yet how to continue with a piece of me now missing so I will think of him jamming with Jaco* and petting his Otis*. Information on services will be forthcoming.

(Jaco refers to Jaco Pastorius, American Jazz Bassist and Otis, his cat that died in 2011)

Chapter 1

Beginnings

I had a special connection with my son from the moment he was born. I realize most mothers do and I did with my other children too but not like this. The best way to explain it is that *I already knew him*. He was my easiest birth and I did all of my births naturally and with no drugs whatsoever so I was clear headed at the time. When he was born and they laid him on my chest I actually said, whether audibly or not I don't now recall, "I know you". I truly feel that if he would have been put among a hundred other babies I would have been able to pick him out, the connection was so strong and I knew his face. We had not learned the sex of the baby nor had I even had an ultrasound ahead of time so I hadn't even formed any ideas about his looks prior to birth. It just grew stronger from there.

I had lots of experience with children from about age three and up but not with babies and my mom and mother-in-law, at the time, were both eight hours away in different directions. I was in a place with no friends or other relatives so new Mom and Dad were on their own. I had read gobs of literature ahead of time. I was nursing, using cloth diapers, had the coolest Swedish stroller, my nephew's hand-me-down car seat, and anxiously awaited the breast pump's arrival before I headed back to work. Unfortunately I had no clue about sleeping or that average babies did it! John was a lively baby, was fun, giggled, was healthy, nursed well, wasn't odd with people but he didn't sleep. It was typical if he slept five-hours at night, waking to nurse, and maybe two or three fifteen minute naps during the day.

The thing is I thought that was normal because I had no reference so I never questioned it. I just managed it. I was teaching elementary school in inner city Philadelphia at the time so I often cuddled up with him to nurse and fell asleep so I could get some shut eye and be able to teach the next day. I needed to be up by 6am to get ready but John would be sure I was up by 5am. We rented a little house right by a busy road then so I'd take him, bleary-eyed, to the front window and we would sit on the couch. I'd prop him up to see out so he could look at the cars passing by. I used the time to teach him colors and types of vehicles, partly to avoid falling asleep. I'd drone on, "blue car, white truck, and red car " and on and on. It's funny, many years later on the porch of our current home the kids and I spent hours on the porch swing playing a variation on that theme and guessing what color the next car would be coming over the hill and keep score of who got the most guesses correct. I have a tendency to make games out of things as often as possible. Anyway, he'd be entertained for about an hour and doze off long enough for me to dress for work.

We had found a wonderful babysitter, Bridget, who would keep John in her home while I worked. I hated the idea of leaving him, but not having him in a large care facility was a relief to me. Occasionally there were two little girls who were there with him and they were sweethearts who loved to help take care of "baby John". Bridget cared greatly for John and her husband, Ron, was a blessing as well. At one point during the almost two school years he spent there, Ron lost his job and his comment was, "well, now I can spend more time with John".

On the occasions he did sleep he had to fall asleep holding a part of you, a thumb, an ear or your nose. I carried him in a baby backpack to get necessary things done sometimes and the baby swing was a lifesaver. One of the oddest things was that if he happened to fall asleep after about 11:30 am it took at least until midnight for him to fall asleep that night, so all appointments had to be made early because the car was an instant knock out most of the time. It was suggested that we try letting him cry it out a few nights when he had passed the one-year mark. I wasn't thrilled with the idea but I did like the thought of putting him to bed without the long drawn out process. After three nights of projectile vomiting, panic, shaking and extreme sweating I ceased to do what I felt was sheer torture to a child who was not able to cognitively comprehend what was trying to be accomplished. I simply stated when asked, "I can guarantee I won't have to stay with him until he falls asleep at college, it's not a big deal really". You know, I never did have to go to his dorm room and stay with him until he fell asleep. Also, none of my children are still nursing either! Sleep remained a big problem for him for years. John and I flew to see my parents in Pittsburgh just about the time he was one. We stayed at my mom's house. I had explained the "falling asleep too late in the day" issue but she kept suggesting that if he got over tired that might be why has was having a hard time sleeping at night. I love my mom and we get along wonderfully. She is very knowledgeable and a great deal of the good things I know about raising kids came from her, but on this one I challenged her. We made a deal. I told her that if I tried it her way and let him fall asleep that afternoon then she had to promise to stay up with me until he was asleep for the night. She agreed. I knew she wouldn't go back on her word. Although she might regret it! We went about a day of silliness and fun. Of course John zonked later that afternoon. Well, at about 1:00 am Mom was quite surprised and saying she had never seen a baby like John. The rest of the trip she helped make sure he never dozed after late morning again. She is awesome and we still joke about the story. His sleep issues continued throughout his life in different forms.

He was an extremely affectionate baby and loved being cuddled. He moved constantly and was extremely curious. He crawled at seven months and walked at nine months.

He climbed, oh how he climbed. Having a high chair for John served only as a simulated mountain to climb up into and out of. He preferred to sit in a mini-rocking chair that his dad's coworkers had made at his birth. It worked well being scooted up to the coffee table to serve as his eating spot, coloring place etc. It worked out fine as the rented house was small and had no formal eating area. Trying to *make* John do certain things would sometimes result in a very disturbing practice he started. It wasn't the typical toddler tantrum I had seen many times before. He would show signs of beginning to get frustrated or upset and fall to his knees, lean back slightly then hurl forward to bang his head on the floor. It got so I could read the signs and I'd slide like a base runner and get my hand, palm-up, under his forehead just in time to cushion the slam. It could be anything. Putting him in the highchair rather than the rocker to eat, peeling a banana "wrong", shoes feeling "weird". Usually it was things that don't faze average kids. These are things that were all beginnings to more difficult challenges later on in his life. They were also things that began to drive wedges between his father and me.

It is very easy for a married couple to be stressed about children but when they have difficult behaviors it is inevitable. He felt that I needed to stand firm and not give in and that John would straighten up. I was not a push over and I stood my ground on most things but I knew in my heart there was something to these behaviors. When it came to picking up toys he had two choices, pick up the toys or get a spanking and pick up the toys. My other two kids will certainly remember those directions because they were the same for many situations when they had issue with my directive. I was firm when it was needed but I looked at situations and thought "is it necessary to get upset by this". I tried to preempt what I could. If I knew cutting food would be an issue, that it somehow bothered him I would slow down, ask him how he'd like it.

I wasn't catering to him but preventing a meltdown. I was also letting him know that I understood that somehow this was an issue and I'd try to lessen that for him. I developed a sense of anticipation. It wasn't a burden; it became second nature to me. Maybe it was because I was so in tune with him it was almost like I could feel it coming at times. I wanted to help my son. It wasn't about avoiding conflict it was about coping, both for him and me. I didn't realize it at the time but it was the beginning of helping him to develop coping skills and strengthening our bond to lean on one another for strength.

He had an obsession with airplanes the way some kids do with dinosaurs. He would do this with many other things as he grew as well. It began early, partly because his dad had begun taking private pilot lessons and because of books. We lived near Willow Grove Air Force Base, which was still active at the time, and he had gotten so good at identifying planes from their underbelly that when he heard one fly over he'd beg to run outside. He'd look up he'd yell A-10 or whatever was going overhead. A-10's were his favorite.

He had several Matchbox style warthogs that loved playing with. He knew what a windsock for an airport looked like and if he spotted one from the road there was no going past. You had to pull over or into the airport to at least see an airplane or hope for a take off or landing. It became one of those head banging situations so if we saw one coming and there was no time I'd do my best to distract him in hopes that he wouldn't see it. Imagine if your kid was into dinosaurs and they still walked around and you had to stop every time you saw one or thought you might! He loved the occasional flight he got to take with his dad.

We also had an Oshkosh video that showed all kinds of planes. He especially loved the aerobatic pilots doing tricks. He wanted to watch the video endlessly. John was just shy of two now. I had bought a small teddy bear in anticipation of a second baby's arrival in a few months so John suggested a name for the bear. He said, " His name is Yurgis, like Yurgis Karris, the aerobatic pilot from the a-planes movie". He called them a-planes instead of airplanes. He did things like this all the time. It stopped you in your tracks and made you roll laughing at the same time. Yurgis bear became his brother's favorite but went by the common name "bear". John had a tiny bear he named 18-19 because he liked those numbers. There was an identical one he called "baby's 18-19" for the baby.

He had an uncanny ability to remember anything he heard after only two or three times on television or in a movie. That was a nasty winter and Philadelphia City schools were closed for almost the entire month of January in '94 due to ice and we were commenting on the ice buildup outside the kitchen door and he chimed in "You need Ice Melt, buy it at Lowes", with energetic inflection, sounding just like the spot played on the weather channel. We would often have to put away Disney movies for a time because during the third time they were played he would recite them as they played and it could nearly drive you crazy.

During the ages one to three I have to say things are not cut and dried clear probably because my second son, Ethan was born when John was twenty-two months old. Ethan was an uncomplicated pregnancy, pretty simple birth and John was thrilled to have a brother. He only seemed upset once when I was holding Ethan and he pointed at the bassinette and said "baby back". He wanted me to put his brother back so he could have me to himself for a while. Other than that Ethan was "his" baby, "his" brother. He wanted to be wherever his brother was. There aren't too many pictures of baby Ethan without John in them as well. He came in May and that fall I didn't return to teaching. I loved being a mom at home. Although exhausting and still without family or friends anywhere near, I had my boys. Because of the experience with John I would wake Ethan up from naps! Yes, still not realizing babies slept I'd wake up Ethan but began finding it odd that he was sleepy so I started to let him sleep more.

Ethan wanted nothing more that to keep up with his brother. So much so that he crawled at five months and walked at seven. Fortunately the little house was just that, little. I would let him nap more than John but was still afraid to let him fall asleep too late in the day. Around three o'clock the boys liked to watch C.H.i P.s on one of the few stations we got. They liked to watch the motorcycles basically. Then they would start to doze so to prevent sleeping they would have bath time. They would play in the tub together, have a blast and wake up. Most people relax their kids in the tub but I used it as a wake up tool. It also made for less of a hassle not having to bathe them at night, less rush. John loved being naked and that helped make him easy to potty train and he was out of diapers by 26 months.

That was especially nice since I used cloth for both boys. Ethan was a very clingy baby and very snuggly. I called him my barnacle boy. He had beautiful big green eyes that could melt your heart. He was his brother's shadow and John adored him just as much. Ethan had some speech delays and called John, Nonny. John called Ethan, E and did his whole life.

Evan Coller > John Van Horn
August 4 at 12:59 am

Man I couldn't believe it when I heard it. I still can't. I remember all the times we were sitting on the porch playing poker and Monopoly. All the camps we went to together. Dude, I'm gonna miss seeing you around. You were a great friend and always had the ability to make people laugh. I hope you're enjoying it up there, jamming out some crazy tunes

Maggie Keener
August 4 at 10:35 am

John, I can't say I remember when we first met because I was just a baby. But I do remember running around both of our houses as kids and always having fun playing with you and your siblings. We drifted apart as we grew up but the day my best friend told me she was dating you I was so excited t see you again. I'm so glad I got to reconnect with you in recent years. You're the type of person that makes everything a party, your laugh is contagious and your goofy smile can't help but make everyone around you smile as well. I'll miss you. I'll miss getting your random hilarious snapchats. I'll miss knowing you're always the person I can count on to be down for whatever. I know you're up there making heaven a party, rock on.

Tom Gordon > Jon Van Horn
August 4 at 11:38 am

I still can't grasp the reality that you are no longer with us. But my heart has peace knowing that you are now in a place with no more pain. God must have needed a little more punk in his life because he called you home way too early. Life has taken us on different paths over the recent years but as I think of you there are so many memories that flood into my mind. One of the best ones being when we were in Pittsburgh for the concert and the security officers told our moms that Club Zoo was for young people. You will live on in all of our memories and in the lives of those that your donations will save. I look forward to the day that I will se you again in glory. Thank you for being a part of my life.

Knowledge

I didn't know
I could love that much
Until I touched your soft skin
For the very first time

I didn't know
I could care that much
Until I eased your tears
During the difficult times

I didn't know
I could laugh that much
Until I laughed with you
Every single time

I didn't know
I could feel music that deeply
Until I heard you play
And it happened all the time

I didn't know
I could feel pride like that
Until I saw the man you became
In such a short time

I didn't know
I could feel heartbreak like this
Until I touched your soft skin
For the very last time

Michelle 2015

Adam Sheetz
August 4 at 4:54 pm

It's hard to wrap my head around it, but it is with terrible sadness that I say, my cousin John has passed away, and far too soon before his time. I wish so very much that I got to spend more time with him as he grew into the awesome young man he became, and I wish I got to play music with him, even just once, like we had talked about. Evelyn, Ethan, aunt Michelle, Carol Sue (Grammy), and Grandpa Gus, I wish I could be there to hug all of you. I love you.

Kristen Kucia
August 6 at 2:08 pm

A very special #tbt, for my cousin Johnny who passed away this Monday. I still cannot believe you are gone. Johnny always had me laughing when we were together. I have so may fond memories of holidays and camping trips spent together that I will cherish forever. RIP Johnny.

Tamara Jackson Coller > John Van Horn
August 4 at 7:04 am

Little Johnny Van Horn, the cute golden haired boy that shared lots of summer days on my porch playing Legos and boards games, You grew up into a handsome great guy, I was so proud of all of your accomplishments. I take comfort knowing that you are with our Lord and as an organ donor you gave selfless to others.

Ryan Deleon
August 4 at 9:57 am

I still find it weird how that butterfly can to chill and smoke a bowl with me that late at night. I believe it was John Van Horn sticking by his word by coming up this month to visit. I've learned to understand life and how everything works around it because of you John. I'm gonna miss you so much.

Chapter 2

Growing

As John passed toddler years I kept an eye on the little things like the head banging, which changed as he got more verbal and was better able to express thoughts. He still got very flustered, well more than flustered, frustrated, but I wouldn't say angry. He wasn't an angry child but he could not put into words what he was feeling. I'd comment sometimes it was like he alternated between a sad year and a happy year. It wasn't as though he was sad all the time but it was as though you could tell he was carrying a weight he shouldn't have been. He was still extremely active and social.

We moved to the Central Pennsylvania town of Bellefonte when the boys were three and one at the opportunity to buy my late grandparents home. Bellefonte is a beautiful Victorian town about twelve miles from Penn State's main campus. A few months before John turned five his sister Evelyn arrived, again there was nothing but a positive reaction from him and Ethan. They both were protective and thrilled to have a sister. As a matter of fact there was a wonderful John story attached to it. You see he had blue eyes, but his brother, father and I all have green so ever since he could express it he insisted his eyes were green like everyone else in the family and would hear nothing to the contrary. The day his sister was born he came to the hospital, climbed into the bed beside Evy and me, took one look at her and said,

"She has blue eyes, just like me". I have had many people tell me that I have been very fortunate because they have never seen children as close as mine have been to each other. I have been truly blessed.

John began showing a great deal of difficulty with doing things like leaving for the store without enough warning, or erratic scheduling and over stimulation and some types of concentration. This is also the year I began homeschooling his kindergarten year. After several anxiety attacks, for lack of a better word, when running late for swimming lessons at the YMCA or getting together with friends I finally concluded that John needed to really have advanced warning and preparation for leaving his comfort zone. So I got into the habit of reminding him the night before of what would be happening the next morning/day. Then giving at least an hour's notice and 15-minute updates for leaving time. This dropped his anxiety level quite a bit. He didn't really have a problem being with others. As a matter of fact he loved other people, adults included. Once we got to where we were going he was fine. He was willing to try all kinds of things, out of the ordinary things and meet new people.

My rule with the kids has always been that if you want to find out something YOU have to do it or call or ask, (thanks Mom). Once when Ethan, understand he is the shy child, got a new Lego set for Christmas and there was one crucial piece missing. I told him if he wanted to get the piece replaced he would need to call the company in Sweden and tell them the problem and ask for a replacement. He reluctantly did and got the new piece. It actually turned out to be an exciting, confidence-building moment. It's always been the same rule. You can't always depend on Mom or others to do it for you. All three of my kids have done very well with this. No speech anxiety, very little fear of unfamiliar situations and they all are pretty self-assured.

By this time John had begun making friends (me too). At swimming we were meeting several other families who were teaching their children at home and this was a great opportunity to plan for the boys to play at other times. It just so happened that the group was loaded with boys! We hit it off with one family in particular who had three boys right around my boys' ages. They have remained friends for just shy of 20 years now. Around the same time John became friends with a boy down the street and we all met a young man, Daniel, neither, of which were homeschooled. Daniel would baby-sit occasionally and ended up becoming like another member of our family and still remains as such. So John was never isolated from other children by being homeschooled as these are only some of the closest friends he made during his youngest years. He still enjoyed time with his brother most and they spent hours together building with Legos and having countless other adventures in their little shared room.

Chapter 3

Personal Revelations

Not long after Evelyn's birth I began to have what I thought was a great deal of post partum depression so I spoke to our family doctor. He was the doctor for all five of us and knew our family dynamic, which was helpful. I hadn't felt down or agitated or on edge after the births of my boys but three is a big change. My now-ex-husband had recently taken a job that sent him away in the summers for up to six weeks at a stretch then home for three then gone for five weeks the first year Evy was born. She came in April and he left at the beginning of July. It was a job that allowed for no contact while he was away. Still far enough from family, and my parents were still working full-time, I was on my own. Both my mid-wife and family doctor suggested an antidepressant and I began taking it.

I'll give a little background on my relationship. It was not always the best and it made for struggles. Because we agreed that I would stay home with the children, and I was grateful for that, there was an expectation that I was to be a real life June Cleaver. Tried as I did, no human I have ever met can keep a perfect spotless house, yard, make a flawless dinner and have perfectly behaved children while also educating them with no help or encouragement. In all honesty many of the interactions were criticisms. Although I didn't give any reason to believe otherwise I was not trusted to grocery shop and was brought home groceries with which to prepare meals, then criticized for not being creative enough with them. I asked for money for essentials like milk and bread as necessary.

Because he was the money-earner he considered it "his money". It was a critical environment but I continued to tell myself that if I tried harder I would please him and be successful. There were rises and falls in intensity over the years, details of which I won't give at this point.

Frequent quarrels and shouting really bothered John. He could see how much the berating affected me and he became more protective of me. His personality was one of compassion and things affected him deeply. I tried very hard not to make negative comments about his dad but instead would express to John that when he was a husband that he was to respect his wife and love her. He was to help her do things and although she should know how to do things like cook and clean he must offer to help her and she should offer to help him do his jobs too. At the same time I told my daughter if you get married your husband should do x, y and z for you but you need to know how to do them yourself and then she learned how to change a dead battery in the store parking lot when she was six alongside the boys. The children and I also had become active in a very nice church and met many wonderful families who cared about our wellbeing. I took opportunities for John and the other children to spend time with strong families that had good marriages so they would see examples of how husbands and wives should interact. John was given the chance to go hunting a few times with friends and their dads and uncles and have great connections with good men. I do believe all of these little things had a positive impact on him a bit at a time.

As John grew we became more alike in personality, which brought us closer and helped me understand him better. Our humor matched and we just clicked on so many levels. Unfortunately I believe this further drove a wedge between him and his father. The things that annoyed his father about me were so similar in John as well and this made it more difficult for him to enjoy John. I frequently use humor to lighten the mood when possible and I saw John beginning to do the same. He was good. He could let things roll off his back better than I could. I envied that.

In the midst of all of this I gained significant weight. This occurred during the three-year period after Evy was born. I had been about 124lbs. when I met my spouse at 18. After my third baby was born at 29, I settled back in at about 123lbs. At 5'3" that wasn't a bad weight. My ex liked to jokingly poke my belly and say you look fine just don't let "that" get any bigger. He used to express that there was no reason I couldn't weigh 118 lbs. Meanwhile he weighed in, well, at a lot more than college weight. I had ballooned to 189lbs. and was devastated. I never had a weight problem, even pregnant. It was clear I was not attractive to my mate and I felt lousy. I finally did research and saw the doctor to find out that my antidepressant had basically turned off my metabolism. He took me off of it. I'd also been experiencing some pretty bad anxiety, mood issues, extreme irritability and irrational thoughts along with a myriad of other unsettling things. When I tried to discuss it with my ex he would tell me it was in my head and to quit thinking about it. He also enjoyed using it against me during arguments. When he would get me to confide in him and let my emotions out it would all get thrown back at me so I never knew what topic was safe to discuss. I thought I was going crazy and he assured me that I was. Things just got worse and the more I read and thought back to my childhood/teen frustrations and talked to my doctor we both felt that I was exhibiting bipolar illness. He chose to hold off on meds a little bit until the old ones were completely cleared out of my system but gave me his home number in case of an emergency. I spiraled from there and remember over that next week it was a blur of panic and rock bottom. I really can't explain. One evening I recall lying on the attic floor feeling unable to will myself to move. It was extremely hot but I couldn't do it. John came up the stairs and reminded me that they had karate practice and I said that his dad was just going to have to take them for once. He came back a few minutes later and told me dad had said to tell "psycho mom to snap out of it" but I told John I couldn't do it. He told me it was ok Mama and that he was old enough that he and Evy could walk the 6 blocks. (This is not a dangerous town and it was summer daylight) His dad finally broke down and took them that one time. I, never wanting to impose on his personal space, called my doctor at home probably incoherent. I remember sitting on the floor between my bedside and the wall shaking and rocking explaining that I knew I wouldn't make it more than a day or two, I couldn't take anymore. I would only hang on for the kids. He told me to come in. I was in a shaking daze for the remainder of the day. I just glazed through the argument that ensued and functioned as I could.

The appointment day I had to step it up because my ex had a bunch of motorcycle off-road expedition riders coming for a weekend gathering and I needed to be a good hostess and do preparations and still get to the doctor's office, but now I had hope. At the appointment he prescribed me both an anti-depressant and mood stabilizer. He chose an anti-depressant in a different family than the old one so it would not cause the weight gain issue to continue. He also instructed me to get in with a psychiatrist right away to both verify what we were both thinking and for therapy. I filled the script on the way home with a voucher, as it would be an expensive endeavor. A huge sense of relief washed over me on the long drive home. Although I knew it was no easy fix, finally someone believed me and wanted to help. Because of insurance issues and the fact that it was "my problem" I had to find creative ways to get into a psychiatrist with my own money, which came from yard sales, doing evaluations for homeschooling families once a year (a requirement in Pennsylvania) sewing projects and other things. There is a county system here that does sliding scale payment and they were willing to use only my income as the base after I explained. I got in to see probably the only psychiatrist I've ever felt comfortable with and have completely trusted. I stayed with him for nearly eight years until he retired, which was a heavy blow.

After a good deal of personal history gathering, discussion and medical history he agreed wholeheartedly with my family doctor's diagnosis and with the medications he had chosen. Huge smile, except that I didn't want to "be bipolar". I met with Dr. Burke as often as I could afford to. I researched bipolar and did crazy amounts of legwork to get into patient assistance programs to get both of my medications affordably. One medication came from the manufacturer at $10 for a three-month supply and the other was free. This was an unbelievable blessing, as they together would have exceeded $800 a month, which would have meant, no medication. In a few short weeks I noticed a significant difference in how I felt and in my moods and many of the other "features" of bipolar illness as it manifested itself in me. Also, since coming off of the old anti-depressant the extra weight began to fall off with very little effort since my metabolism kind of restarted. When I saw that happening I got excited and became more active, which accelerated its effect. Within ten months I lost seventy-five pounds. I had managed to hit that 118lb dream weight someone had for me but now my nickname was sometimes "skeletor" because I was too skinny. Anyway, I felt better physically and could run around and my feet didn't ache and I felt better in my clothes and in my own skin.

The kids were proud of me and they lovingly look back at the rare photos I have kept of "fat Mom" and they say they don't even remember my being fat. I think it's because kids look past appearance many times when they love or are being loved. I do remember at the time saying to the friends of mine that I hoped my kids, especially the boys, would realize that they could choose a mate that might not be the skinniest or most beautiful because they loved them. I also remember envying women I had seen on wedding shows that were heavier when they married knowing they were loved for who they were and they wouldn't have to worry about always being toothpick skinny for fear of being thrown overboard.

Tensions just increased over the years and I do not claim to have been perfect or the perfect mate. I will make that clear. I will probably add to this later but continuation of these behaviors for well over 20 years eventually caused me to decide to divorce my spouse.

Living with this illness has not been a day at the park, but I try to look on the positive side and imagine how much harder it would have been for me to understand my son if I had not also walked a mile in his shoes. I am extremely grateful that the combination of medications I started with was a good fit right from the beginning and that I didn't have to go through a lot of trial and error. Please understand that medication doesn't "cure" bipolar, it helps to manage the symptoms and lessen them. I still have periods of deep lows and doubt. I still feel the anxiety creeping in, but I also feel like it sits under the surface rather than jumping out like a jack-in-the-box. For me, circumstances like stress, sleep, and situational things are triggers and it takes a long time to get it all figured out and I've not figured it all out yet. I feel my illness changing as I age.

At times I am fearful as to what lies before me and if there will be anyone beside me to help me through the dark places but I have to take it one day at a time and always be looking for a purpose and reevaluating my treatment plan. I realize some people who are pretty close to me will read this book and learn of my illness for the first time, but stigma is part of what I'm trying to change with this book. I'm the same person I was before you cracked open this cover. Please remember that.

Daniel Corbett
August 4 at 1:56 pm

Today has been a sad day for the world as a bright and shining life has ended. Watching John Van Horn grow into the man he had become over the past 16 year was an honor and a privilege that I will cherish forever. Though I was not a bold relative I feel like I lost my brother, and with that my heart goes out to Evelyn Van Horn, and Ethan Van Horn., I have to say my favorite memories with him are the amazing Halloween trick-or-treating we did, and the Siamese Twins costume we has that made me feel short because I was 7 years older and he was already taller than me! Michelle Sheetz Van Horn was like my second mother and treated me like one of her own. I love you John. I will miss you. Please keep these people in your thoughts and prayers and send positive energy in this time of sorrow.

Clayton Filipowicz
August 4 at 4:39

Just the kind of guy John Van Horn was. Always would check up on you, even in passing. I remember in high school when he was over at my house, I think I went upstairs for a millisecond and when I came back down he had devoured a box of tasty cakes and was starting in on the pretzels. Haha we have all come a long way since then. Last time I saw him he had lost a ton of weight and seemed to thoroughly enjoying life. It's troubling news to find out he's gone now. He will be missed. That's for sure.

Todd Eisenhauer > John Van Horn
August 4 at 7:27 pm

John Van Horn was legitimately one of the coolest people I have ever known. I'll never forget hanging out with him at his place after football or our mutual love of old school punk. I know Adam L. would agree, nothing would have been as grand if you weren't there for it with us. Nobody had a heart as big as yours.

Mal Veronica > John Van Horn
August 4

John, I'm sitting here on the beach, enjoying this beautiful day. And I can't breathe. I can't believe that you are no longer in this world of oceans and sunshine. I know that life has taken us down different roads in the past couple of years, but I think about you everyday. I remember playing with you on the hill behind the church when we were four years old, and singing with you at youthgroup. I remember the day you got your beloved green shoes… You loved those shoes. I remember how much you helped me when my mom decided to homeschool us and I was having a hard time. We would go to "science class" at the Howard dam and you would sit by Thomas and I and talk to me the whole time. I remember when you and Evy and Ethan and your mom were in a car accident on the way there one time, and I was so worried. I couldn't imagine a world with no John Van Horn. But, I know you are at peace now, and that God has you in his everlasting arms. I can't wait to hear your music again someday when I join you. Play hard for all of us, and I will see you again someday.

Katelyn Lackey > John Van Horn
August 4 at 5:51 pm

Over the past few years we've only run into each other a couple of times, but I have so many good memories with you from when we used to hang out, jam, and play ultimate Frisbee after youth group. You introduced me to School of Rock, influenced my taste in music, and are the reason I love bass so much! You've always been one of the friendliest and most talented people I've had the pleasure to know. As sad as this news is there is joy in the fact that I believe you're having an amazing time with Jesus, singing better music that you've ever known.

Chapter 4

Difficult Dynamics

The relationship between a father and his children varies between children for sure and it was certainly that way between John and his dad and John's siblings. No one was really favored, but John and his dad clashed somehow. John didn't purposely antagonize his dad yet it seemed that his just being there somehow was bothersome at times. John was never an ass-kisser, not that his brother and sister were by any means, but John marched to his own drum and was the most strong-willed of the three. I read The Strong Willed Child by James Dobson and found it very helpful. I think that John figured out on his own that there was truly no way to really please his father and he consciously or unconsciously gave up on that and just lived his life. As I had mentioned earlier John naturally used humor in his everyday life to get through tough situations and to lighten the mood of others.

John had a child-sized motorcycle for a long time and that was a good connection for the two of them and then his dad would take him on the back of his dual-sport bike for off-road excursions until he got a bit too heavy to ride two up. If John was showing interest in an activity that his dad enjoyed, like his motorcycle then all was well but it was really hard for his dad to become interested in activities he didn't value or care for and this was a disappointment for John. Like all children John wanted very much to make his dad proud of him and have his positive attention. Once when he was about five I was tucking him into bed and he said, "maybe someday someone will write a song about Dad" and then he said, "wait, they already have. It's called Cat's in the Cradle". He was an unusually in-tune child. From the time John was nine to about eleven years old I took him to a therapist with the hope that he would learn some other coping skills or that the therapist would be able to give me some other insight into his stressed little mind. I think he found some relief talking in the sessions and it made him feel like he wasn't a bad kid for feeling the way he did sometimes. He said he liked going. The situation did bother his father. Mental health issues were very uncomfortable subjects for him.

John worked very hard to show his best abilities, especially his outstanding musical abilities, which showed up very early. It wasn't until he had been accepted at Lock Haven University to study music education with classical piano as his focus did his dad acknowledge to others that John had musical talent. It always seemed that John couldn't make the grade. In his father's eyes, it could have always been better or faster or earlier, anything other than what it was. The "pet" names for John and me reflected the negative aspect that floated around but John rolled with it. He and sometimes the dog were referred to as "dumb ass". I'll never forget in the kitchen one July my ex commented. "Oh yeah dumb ass has a birthday coming up" and John just calmly retorted, I didn't know Zeus (the dog) is having a birthday?" He just let that stuff roll off. At least it looked like that to others.

The relationship between the two of them never really got to the point of yelling arguments or heated disagreements. It just more or less just sort of got cold you could say. John seemed to be an annoyance to his dad and his dad was a logic puzzle that John couldn't figure out.

Chapter 5

Sports

Daniel, who first started out as the young man who would occasionally watch the kids and had become more of a family friend was very active in Tang So Do karate and John began showing an interest in the sport himself. The kids and I had gone to the YMCA to watch. Several other friends were in the class as well so I brought up the class to his dad. He didn't think much of the idea as he was not a fan of the sport, hadn't done it himself, so he wasn't supportive and suggested that if I was set on it then I would need to fund it. John was about six or seven at this time, was having quite a few self-control issues, frustration problems, irritability and some anxiety. I hoped this might be a good outlet for energy and I learned from Daniel that it taught self-control and many other important skills. I also knew it was a great place to solidify his current friendships and grow new ones. It was wonderful for him and he saw it too.

After starting he commented to me that he felt better and that he understood the "laws and tenants" he had to learn. He took it very seriously and worked hard to move up in rank. This is where he met his best friend of over 15 years, Ben. He continued in the sport and stopped only when he began to play football in ninth grade. He had reached the rank of blue belt with stripe, the next step would have been to train and test for black belt. His sister saw how much he enjoyed it and took classes with him for many years. He tried hockey for a while in his younger years but that worked out about as well for him as it did for Happy Gilmore.

Our family, I should say everyone except John who didn't really have an interest at the time, began slalom Kayaking in about 2007 at the urging of my ex. He had met a charismatic man, Dave Kurtz, at a meeting and found out about an instructional program that he ran not too far from our home so we started what would be quite a wild ride. We started out slowly learning what would become whitewater slalom kayaking, an amazingly exciting and wonderful sport. Evelyn and Ethan both ended up being quite adept and earned coveted spots on different US teams over the years. The four of us enjoyed the competition. It was quite a thing. Well, at one point His dad and I insisted that John take the basic course, which lasted only a few weeks. Our reasoning was that at some point in his life friends would be bound to invite him to go kayaking recreationally and we felt it was important to know how to do it safely and correctly rather than see him floating down the creek haphazardly with a six pack and no safety gear like the yahoos we saw frequently go by and then find in trouble. He agreed and began the course.

Because John was a bit heaver at the time he had to use one of the plastic recreation style boats like his dad rather than the sleeker slalom boats because they have a much smaller capacity and in general max out at about 180lbs. The ones our club owns don't even go that high. So that was a bit of a disappointment for him but he did just fine. He did feel a bit behind since we all were paddling pretty well already but he pressed on. At the completion of the basic course sessions Dave sets a slalom course on the creek for each participant to run in his boat, times you and calculates penalties for each of the two runs. It is the same set up as a race would be. He likes to gather the information for his records and keep running stats of students. So John took his two runs and did just fine.

He was never really big on competition. By the way, if you are not familiar with slalom kayak only one boater is on the course at a time. Then his dad, who had already taken the course mind you and isn't in line for a turn, wants to run the course to see if he can beat John's time. In his first and second run he fails to beat John's time and then refuses to leave the water until he has beaten John's course time. I don't know how many runs it took to finally lay down a faster time, but his dad spent a good long time gloating to John about how he could beat his time. John never wanted to come kayaking with us again.

Although after his ninth grade football season he slimmed down and could fit into one of the larger slalom boats. Ethan convinced him to come down to paddle with just him and his sister. John found the slalom boat to be a lot more fun and agile. He commented that if he had been able to fit into a slalom boat the first time out maybe he would have liked it more and done more with it. Seeing that John was not highly competitive I don't think he would have enjoyed racing at the level his brother and sister did even if he had had the talent necessary. He did enjoy the opportunity to watch Evelyn paddle in the Jr. World Championships the year she was on Jr. team and it was held in Wausau, WI. He always watched both his brother and sister on live feed when they paddled overseas in Jr. and U23 World Championships other years. They couldn't have had bigger supporters than their brother. It reminds me that he tried out his German language skills (he studied two years) on one of the cute German kayak team members and she in turn practiced her English with him while he was in Wisconsin for the race. He crashed and burned, but made a good effort.

John had always enjoyed the sport of football and partly because his paternal grandmother is a diehard Buffalo Bills fan. She has had season tickets since the mid-seventies. He grew up hearing Grandma talk football with the knowledge of a seasoned player turned announcer and she can yell at the television with the best of them. I remember one trip to Buffalo as we walked in the door, a game was on and something bad must have just happened and you heard Grandma in the distance let out a roar. John was probably four and Ethan two. He just kind of looked in the direction of the living room in wonder and Ethan started to cry! He liked watching games with her when possible, always could be heard agreeing with her that "this was their year" and as he got older he would discuss draft picks with Grandma and stats. He had the good fortune to attend two pro games with her. One of the games was Buffalo vs. Pittsburgh. He of course wore his Bills winter coat but under that he had on a Steelers shirt (for mom, being from Pittsburgh). When the Steelers took the lead he unzipped the coat and Grandma got a kick out of it, as did the folks around her. I do believe the Bills won that game.

Well, the summer before he would have started ninth grade he decided he wanted to go out for football. In our area even though ninth grade is in the high school it is it's own team and practices separately. So we popped over to the middle school where they practiced and got the information, as the practices were to begin in the next day or two. We rushed to get his physical and have him ready. The two coaches were terrific and very accommodating. He was the first player to be a homeschooled student. Many other homeschooled kids in our district had played baseball, basketball, soccer and such but not football so every now and then when the schedule would change last minute and be moved up an hour or so they'd be on the bus and the coach would be like, "where's Van Horn?" and they'd have to remind him to call the house. We were less than a mile away so it was never disastrous.

Because he had no experience like many of the other boys who had been playing Pop Warner ball for years he didn't get a lot of field time at first but was very "on the ball" and did whatever the coaches wanted. He and another boy, Todd, always got the job of hauling out the down measurement chains and they ended up being called "chains". Coach just had to call out "chains" and he and Todd jumped to it. It wasn't long before he showed enough hard work and ability to be a starter in a game or two. His brother, sister and I attended every game, whether or not he played. It was fun. I remember how much it meant when either one or both of my parents came to things I did. When Daniel heard that John would be playing football that year he went in and told his boss that he would be missing at least one Tuesday night because he had to go see his "brother" play football. His father did attend one of his games and it meant a great deal to John.

He met some new friends that year, he already knew some guys from other places like church or camp and it was funny when he'd share stories with us when he came home. Many of the guys were very intrigued about him "going to school at home". They asked all kinds of questions and he gladly answered and found it amusing. They

Adam Miller
August 4 at 3:43 pm

I am very sorry and saddened to hear that John Van Horn passed away yesterday August 3. Although we hadn't spoken in quite sometime, I remember all the years of Vacation Bible School and youth group when we were younger. His smile was certainly contagious, and he loved to laugh. Every memory I have of him was filled with laughter at some point. I still have some good memories of us playing guitars before and after youth group. We both shared a love and passion for music. I can only imagine the music being played in heaven right now. I will be praying for his family as they grieve the loss of a brother, son, and friend. I ask that my friends pray with me. John you will be missed, and I wish we had the chance to jam one more time.

Ed Walls
August 4 at 2:45 am

Hard to believe you're gone. I'll always remember this day fondly: the day we played to a packed chapel at Camp K as "The Final Hour". Rest easy, John.

Sara Michelle Bowling
August 4 at 4:42 pm

I am so sorry to hear that my friend John Van Horn has passed away. I can't remember a time that I wasn't laughing when you were around. Your smile and love for music were infectious. Rest Easy.

Erin Nilson
October 9

Even though he's not here to thank in person, I know he can hear me. When I'm driving home and listening to a certain song that makes me sad, I can hold onto his guitar pic around my neck or glance down at his signature on my arm and hear him tell me it's all going to be all right as long as we have each other. It will be all right, because I still do have you forever. Thank you John Van Horn, just for being the beautiful you.

wanted to know if he ever left the house, had to get dressed, had friends, actually did school work and all sorts of things. He really educated them about what his life was like and sometimes he would mess with them. Most of them envied the fact that once a week we had "jammas day" when they could wear their pajamas all day.

Because I was a substitute teacher in the district it was amusing to go into a classroom at the high school and have a bunch of boys say, " Aren't you John's mom?" and when I'd say I was every football player that came in the room would hear, "that's John's mom". I always felt very blessed that John never went through the stage of being embarrassed that I was his mom. Whenever I dropped him off or picked him up somewhere he'd give me a big hug and kiss in front of people and tell me he loved me, audibly. He liked to introduce me to his friends and smile and say, "This is my mom". It always made me feel so special, like I must not have messed up too badly yet or have been too hideous! I liked being known as "John's Mom".

He decided not to play his tenth and eleventh grade years but did want to for his senior year. When it was time for the season to begin the rest of the family would be out of town so I arranged for him to have dinner with several different families occasionally so he wasn't totally on his own and I made sure he was set to go to football camp. As things tend to go sometimes, on the first practice play of football camp John took a hit. It wasn't overtly hard because there were no paint mark on the new white helmet he wore, but it must have been one of those hits that were just right, or wrong. He didn't play anymore that day. That night it was determined he had a concussion. I think he was almost more disappointed that he didn't get to ride the roller coasters at the theme park later that week than getting hit. When we got home I took him to see a neurologist. He did a scan and asked John and me questions. His memory had been poor for over a week. He'd play a Playstation game with Ethan and then when Ethan asked what he wanted to play next and John answered Ethan would say, "That's what we just played", lots of things like that. When it was all said and done he laid it out for John. He let him know the risks of another head injury at his age, possible instant death if he received another blow within two months, explained how learning and retention would most likely be difficult for several months, especially in mathematics and more. He asked what position john played and John told him, linebacker and that it was part of his job to get hit. I wanted to scream for him not to play but I needed him to decide that. I looked at him and said, "What do you think?" John said, "I have enough trouble with math already, but more than that, I think it's a risk I shouldn't take." I was relieved.

We were heading directly back to the high school because the team was lifting and John felt it was his obligation to tell the coach and hoped he would not be letting him down. We got there and he asked me to come in with him. Coach Wyncoop came out to meet him right away and almost in tears John told him he wouldn't be able to play and he added that he'd like to still be a part of the team somehow if that were possible. The coach told him he understood and was hoping very much that he would still want to be a part of things and gave him a hug. John was given management duties and also began to participate in lifting as soon as he was medically cleared to do so. The other guys were very accepting of the situation. He still had to meet academic requirements like everyone else for the season, he was honored like everyone else on senior night and during the football banquet Coach said some very kind words and awarded him a letter for his service.

Chapter 6

Church, Youth Group and Camp Years

The kids and I had become active in a local church when John was about six or seven. We all knew quite a few people there and it really started out with a summer of attending Vacation Bible School, VBS. It was a wildly energetic, active week of daylong activity that John thrived on. He became very interested in learning about scripture and loved attending weekly Sunday school/church and youth activities on Wednesday nights.

His desire to be a compassionate boy was encouraged here and he learned a great deal about the love Jesus showed for all people and I think that whether or not he was attending a church at the time of his death, what he drank in spiritually all those years helped build the amazing man he became. He prayed to receive Christ as his savior as a young boy and renewed this prayer as a teen with excitement during summer camp one year. I remember one winter Sunday when John was about 10, we woke up to quite a lot of snow and John went out and shoveled the driveway without being asked, to be sure we wouldn't miss getting to church. As he got too old to participate in VBS he started to be a helper with the younger kids. The little kids really took to him and he did so well with them. He was a gentle soul and was so sweet to them.

There was a man in our church who had become disabled after a blood infection and was basically in need of constant care and could not do even the smallest task himself and his wife needed to have a tiny respite so she asked John if he'd be willing to care for her husband for the three hours of VBS time. It would require him to feed, bathe using a

mechanical lift and dress him (there would be another trained person with him). He had his heart set on hanging with his friends and helping at VBS that week but he very kindly said he'd be glad to do it. He was sixteen or seventeen that year I believe. It was a very humbling experience and very emotional. I think there were a lot of things John didn't take for granted for a very long time after that.

We had and still do have a great radio station that broadcasts a Christian kids show each afternoon that the kids all loved listening to. It gives children chances to call in and answer scriptural questions to win "pogs"(generically called milk caps, is a game that was popular during the mid1990's). He loved calling in. This station also runs a summer camp and when he learned about it he was set on going as soon as he was old enough. I saved up and he went when he was seven. I wrote a letter everyday so he would get mail. Even ahead of time so there would be a letter on the first mail day. He quickly became know as the mail boy. When it came time to pick him up he was already set on going two weeks the next year. As the years passed he applied for "need" scholarships and was able to attend twice a summer and as soon as all three kids were old enough I volunteered as a counselor to get a discount. I loved the time out there myself too. When he was in his teens he volunteered during a week of kids camp on the maintenance crew and camped during youth quest week. He went from ages seven to eighteen.

It became an extremely happy place for him, a place where he was fully accepted and loved. Where he had friends and could express himself and where he felt comfortable. One year at camp he made a tee shirt that said, "move out to Camp K" and I think he would have if he'd had the opportunity. One year his birthday fell right in the middle of the week of Youth Quest and I wondered if he would rethink being away from home for it. Nope, he was more than happy to celebrate after he returned. He wouldn't have missed his week for

anything. I think it is really hard to explain his feelings

for Camp Kanesatake and trying to wouldn't do him justice. I ponder sometimes about spreading a tablespoon of his ashes out at camp so he finally can move out to camp K in a way. Maybe I will someday. Kid's Camp and Youth Quest had great meaning to him as he grew up. I know that he had very deeply meaningful experiences there, great time with friends but private moments of growth as well. You could see the impact it had when he came home and he'd occasionally share some things. I'm grateful that he had those experiences. Several years he took his bass and helped with worship music and during skit time. He went to a guys' retreat one or two winters. He came home eager to show us his aptitude for tie tying. He said they practiced until they could tie them in the bunkhouse in the dark and get it right. Each year at camp they focused on a different scripture verse as the theme but one year they did the entirety of Psalm 1 and he was very excited to come home having memorized the whole thing. His lifelong friend, Thomas, who had been at camp with him that week, read Psalm 1 at John's service.

Chapter 7

Educational Years
Homeschool Years

Our school days were filled with fun and learning, whether it be silly stories, dancing, adventures with stuffed animals, computer CD programs or doing regular work in books, generally we were enjoying our time together. If you ever played Oregon Trail with Ethan never ford the river because it always ended in tragedy, and John was so disappointed to find out that Borax was just soap and not a miracle drug. Having a degree in elementary education I was really excited to begin teaching John, and eventually the others, at home. From the time he was small I had been informally teaching him colors, numbers and all the things most kids learn as they are growing but now that he was five it became a bit more structured.

Although I have always been a strong believer in learning through play during the

early primary years of school there are certainly things that have to be officially taught. I came up with specific reading, math and handwriting exercises for him to do each day. He didn't seem to have phonemic awareness and didn't sound out words. He knew the sounds of letters, but wasn't able to phonetically connect. I found it odd and that became a different set of challenges. So I set out to use sight words as a base for him. He already knew his alphabet and I had been playing with him using two boxes of flash cards with a picture on one side and the word on the other: dog (picture)/dog (word) for a long time since I had them left over from the classroom and he thought they were fun. Anyway, I quickly found that he could be shown a word and told what it was without a picture only a few times and he would remember what it was.

I thought I was doing a great job teaching him, ha ha, it was just John. I began making sight word lists for him of common and useful words and we would practice them. In less than three months he was able to read by himself. It made it difficult to sound out words without my help but eventually he seemed to be able to associate words he knew with parts of words he didn't and figure them out. I found a great system a year or so later that worked great with him called Sing, Spell, Read and Write. It put things to music and helped things that had eluded him prior click for him.

He loved reading and always had books around and he had been read to pretty much since birth. He was thrilled to get books as gifts and my mom was terrific at doing just that. We have several Time Life children's nature series sets that were great additions to our library. He wanted to know everything and I generally would answer his questions of, "Mom how does...?" With, " I'm not sure. How can we find out?" even if I knew the answer. He became a researcher and question asker and eventually a walking encyclopedia. He loved sharing facts and information. He got along with and would talk to anyone, anywhere. He loved the Titanic and learned everything he could about it and one time at a church dinner, when he was about seven, he over heard a group of five or so men discussing the subject. He walked right up to them and excused himself politely and said he was a big fan of the Titanic and asked to join the conversation. They welcomed him and he quickly chimed in with a statistic.

He never saw age difference as boundary. He had respect for those older than himself but felt that they had much to offer him and yet he might be able to offer them something as well.

Reading remained a life-long passion. It was a goal of mine to build a great reference library and it was accomplished over the years. He looked forward to taking a good share of the books with him someday. His favorite books were non-fiction. We visited the public library frequently and he was so very proud of his first library card. The library guidelines required that you could not have your own card until you could sign it by yourself. I still have that card. He went to the librarian one visit when he was still early elementary age, asking for books on World War II, a favorite, and she told him the Dewey Decimal section numbers in the juvenile area. He thanked her and said he'd prefer the adult section please. He was a ravenous reader and we also did a read aloud time each day even through high school. He quite enjoyed the year he studied English poetry and took it upon himself to borrow the complete works of, as the kids like to say in a goofy voice, George Gordon Lord Byron, from the library. He also chose to read Milton's Paradise Lost in Old English so he could "get the full effect". I think it took him twice as long because he had to keep looking up definitions and translations.

He didn't spell well and traditional spelling books never worked for him so I ended up coming up with my own. He could look at a word and tell you it was spelled incorrectly but couldn't spell from scratch. This was a serious point of frustration for him and often hindered his desire to write. We got creative. Between the exercises I had come up with and learning how to use "spell check" to look up words and after the fact on papers as he got older he overcame the frustration.

When it came to writing he would get extremely uptight and have to take frequent breaks. He could form letters just fine and do his penmanship lessons but when it came to writing thoughts he became very agitated, bang the table and I have to tell him to breathe and he'd lift his arms above his head and take a breath and let his arms down and try again. The process was kind of cute. After trial and error I figured out his mind was just moving so much faster than his hand could ever go so I'd have him dictate to me and I'd record it. He still learned to write but this way the extreme frustration was gone and he didn't despise composition. As he got older I let him type his assignments and this worked beautifully.

Math was pretty good overall. He did a lot of building and discussing. When it came to drill and practice we'd go through flash cards in the living room. I show him a card and he'd give the answer, spin around and do the next one and this avoided anxiety through his movement. It took a while to figure out the right math workbooks for him. He hated coloring so I immediately knew I didn't need for him to color the pictures on the worksheets. Honestly that's classroom busywork anyway. I eventually found math books with very little extraneous stuff on the pages. No happy-little dogs and curly-ques. These things are great for average kids but were like fireworks going off for John. Eliminating distraction was very important for him. If he was doing something he was interested in doing, like researching volcanoes he'd be focused for hours, seriously, hours. If not redirection was needed and if too much redirection was needed he began doubting his abilities and telling you he was too dumb to do it or that he'd just mess it up anyway.

The kids did a lot of projects instead of always being stuck in a workbook. Ethan and Evelyn had a cardboard box complex in the living room for what seemed to be weeks; with offices that each had a different business run by a different stuffed animal. We had a detailed running story about Ethan's bear that all the kids contributed to. He owned bologna factories worldwide and we marked them on the world map. John built an atomic bomb blast replica in diorama form using a paper towel roll and dryer lint.

We attended homeschool activities at a local state park run by a wonderful ranger who put together events just for our population. We had field day every year with local families and got together almost weekly for many years until kids got bigger and busy with other things.

John had many great experiences with school and of course some run of the mill days too. Not everything can be fun all the time but those days of just the four of us were relaxed and laid back in general. He went through many high interest subjects besides planes of early years and he never dropped interest in any of them. He got hooked on volcanoes and began learning all he could about those. He went trick or treating at six dressed in a volcano costume I had sewn for him complete with a lava and fluff-smoke hat. He would go to people's doors and tell them, while pointing to the hat, "This is my pyroclastic flow". Mom got a few odd looks. He even talked to a professor of volcanology at Penn State on the phone one time after I helped him find the contact information and she sent him copies of personal photos from one of her research expeditions to an active volcano. It was one of the things he thought about studying in college. He once commented that he didn't know what to go to college for because he wanted to learn everything. That was music to my ears since my biggest goal of homeschooling my kids was to instill in them a love of learning. He got hooked on things and had to learn everything he could about each thing. For a while it was weather. You could say it looked like rain and he'd go out and analyze the clouds to verify or disprove the likelihood of that. He had an affinity for rocks and I still have most every rock he ever gave me. If his siblings went somewhere for a race I'd pick up a rock that looked unusual and take it home. There was always something new and interesting in his world.

John had a huge passion for sharks and every year other things took a back seat to "Shark Week" on the Discovery Channel. I loved watching it with him and he would spit out facts along with the narrators. His favorites were hammerheads and I got a smiling hammerhead shark tattoo on my left shoulder with his signature under it a few months after he died as a happy memorial.

As he got older he would go on "grand tangents" and when I'd ask what he was doing he'd say he had been looking up something like, when the Cuisinart company was established but that made him wonder where X happened, which made him wonder when Y occurred, which made him think about Z and that made him question A, who was married to B but then when did he die and where did they live? It was so interesting to watch his chain of thought. You could see that his mind was just flying all the time and he was chasing to keep up with it. He was in a constant state of thinking.

By high school age he was really good at not believing in himself. He was tremendously talented musically, had a mind filled with a wealth of knowledge, was socially accepted by a variety of people but thought little of himself and his abilities. Most anyone close to him can remember hearing him say at one time or another, "I wish I was good at stuff". He would convince his closest friend at the time, Ben, to go out somewhere because Ben would have much rather stayed in. When they were out Ben would always ask how John knew so many people seeing as he was homeschooled. He usually replied that it was nothing, just someone from, camp or football, or church or any number of places. Ben would just laugh and say he'd been in public school since preschool and didn't know half the people John did.

High School Classes

He had covered a great deal of information at home for school and one of his favorite's would have been his senior year history course, The History of Rock and Roll; 1500-Current Day. He had a great time with that and I really enjoyed gathering the resources. He ended up with a 28-page paper at the end of the year. He obviously didn't have any issues with writing anymore. He had done geometry and chemistry his junior year and I did not feel that I could do justice to trigonometry or physics so he decided he would go up to the high school for those two classes.

Our district is really good about allowing homeschooled students to come in for classes so we set that up. He was scheduled for first and third period classes but they offered for him to stay for a second period study hall so he didn't have to leave and go back so he said yes. When the study hall teacher saw him reading a book on the life of Beethoven and talking to him she asked him to be part of the quiz bowl team. He didn't do it but later said he wished he had joined.

However, each day when he arrived he had to sign in and was so friendly in

the main office that the two secretaries asked if he might like to be an office runner during second period instead of sitting around in study hall. He took that opportunity and because of that almost everyone, students and teachers, got to know him. He was even added among the seniors in the yearbook photos when he wasn't an "official" full time student. It was especially fun to be a sub at the high school that year. I remember covering his trig class and him coming in and giving me a hug and a couple kids asking him if it was weird to have his mom as a teacher. He laughed and told them he'd had me as a teacher everyday since kindergarten. Going in for classes was a good experiencem for him. It made him responsible to someone else in his work besides me. It gave him the chance to take notes during lectures, which didn't happen at home and it was a different teacher to get used to. It also helped me know how to better prepare the other two for post high school pursuits. I joked with him that he was my guinea pig and he'd say, "Thanks a lot", but he ran with it.

He made some new friends that year and he enjoyed the opportunity. We talked a lot about the experience. We talked about how he felt about learning at home versus public school. He was very honest with me, as always. He said he thought it was a good thing he had been schooled at home for a lot of reasons. He told me he felt he was the kind of kid who would have probably been swayed too easily and may have gotten into a bad crowd, may have gotten into a bunch of trouble. He felt he had been given the opportunity to learn more at home and find out more about himself and manage his hard behaviors. "I don't think it would have been good for me there, Mom", he said. He gave me his opinion on how he felt his brother and sister would have fared in public school as well. He had insight well beyond his years. I took everything he said to heart and so much of what he said matched my unspoken thoughts about each of the three of them. Talks like that are some of what I miss most in his absence.

John knew he wanted to continue his education beyond high school but had so many things he wanted to do. He had narrowed it to the air. Sounds pretty wide open but actually he knew that his love of flying had never dwindled so he was thinking about the Navy so he could pursue a career as a pilot. We researched ROTC and he applied to take the required exam. We then looked at all possible colleges where he could get the degree he wanted and decided to dream big because if the ROTC scholarship came through he'd be financially okay. He narrowed it down to three and applied to Purdue, Ohio State and University of Oklahoma. He wanted to GO OU most of all.

Jordan Fye
August 4 at 10:55 am

It's hard to find the right words to explain how something like this could happen to such a kind and loving person. Maybe because there is no good explanation. I spent the last 2 years of my life with John Van Horn and his family. When I wasn't in college or with my family, chances are, I was with John and his family. John was one of my best friends. He was one of the sweetest, most genuine people I've ever met. John had many things that bothered him, but the thing that always got me was that no matter what he was going through, he was always there to help ANYONE. He could have a terrible day and still smile and be there to help you out if you had a problem. There isn't anything I can say that will make you understand how much of a kind, loving person John was unless you knew him. He touched everybody he came in contact with. All because of that big goofy smile and happy-go-lucky attitude. Please pray for John and his family. This is a rough time for everybody that knew him, but I can't begin to imagine what his family is going through. You will be missed John. I love you like a brother man. Rock on buddy.

Marissa Weaver > John Van Horn
August 5 at 3:43 am

Ill' never forget our trig classes together in high school, running into you in Bellefonte ALL the time, attending proms and graduations together, pool parties…and the day I just needed friends to be on my side and you and Erin Rebekah Came to my rescue with the weird movie with the talking cows, pizza, and laughter. I think of these days often and remember them fondly; I will never forget how great of a friend you were to everyone. Thank you.

Lasse Stou > John Van Horn
August 4 at 6:33 pm

I'll always remember John Van Horn as one of the very first people that talked to me when I got to Bellefonte and how he made me feel welcome in a new country. He didn't have to talk to a stranger from Europe and it would probably have been easier to make fun of my name like a bunch of others did… instead he did something pretty amazing, if you ask me, he helped me the best he could to feel welcome and was one of my first American friends. For that I am grateful!

Even though I only spent a year in your company that was more than enough to see what a great and caring person you were. (Even if you were a Sabres fan)
Rest in Peace John.

Alisha Tyler-Lohr
August 4 at 9:14 am

I can't believe the person who was everyone's friend, John Van Horn passed away. May you keep making people smile and laugh. I'll always remember you.

Jadie Click
August 4 at 7:10 am

I will never stop being proud of you. You have an incredible soul, and love everyone around you. I'm so grateful that the last night we hung out we laughed the whole time. I'm going to miss you so much, John Van Horn. Till Valhalla, my brother.

He and his dad had taken a road trip to check it out when I had had surgery and he fell in love with it. He heard from Purdue first, before Christmas and was excited with the acceptance, he was also accepted at Ohio State but was most thrilled with University of Oklahoma's acceptance. It's kind of funny I remember saying to him within a few days after hearing back from Oklahoma. That he would need to find a piano on campus so he could go play when things got stressful and he agreed.

Between application, visit and acceptance he went from thinking about pilot to meteorologist to something else that I don't even remember. When he discovered to what level of calculus you have to study for meteorology and he realized that was out of his reach. At around this time he received word that his score on the mathematical portion of the ROTC exam came in slightly too low to receive a scholarship and that sent everything into rethinking mode. I sat with him and explained that if he had his heart set on Oklahoma he'd still be able to go but would be coming out with large debt. Being a kid who learned early on to be frugal he realized this was not his best choice. He also expressed that he had been really contemplating several things. One was stress and how far he would have been from home to deal with situations, but most of all he said he had been thinking about what he truly loved more than anything, music. He'd been thinking about studying music but wasn't sure what to do with it.

Being a list maker and organizer we started looking into things. We knew he'd be looking at using his piano skills to get accepted somewhere as he had never been formally trained on the bass. We went on line and looked at the list of Pennsylvania state system schools because there are over a dozen of them and are reasonably priced (Penn State is not a PA state system school, it is a semi-private university). We narrowed it down to few schools but focused primarily on Lock Haven University because it was a Steinway School and it happened to be very close by. We found that he could major in music performance or music education. Being a music teacher appealed to him and as our neighbor, a music teacher who helped him prepare a bit, said, "The requirements are similar but in the end if you get the teaching certificate you'll eat".

John and his sister had begun working with a new piano teacher many years prior and we decided to talk to Judy and see if she even though he had a chance. She felt that he truly did and told us to contact the school and find out what needed to be done. We did. He did the regular college application and then was given the requirements for his audition. Judy began working with him on his two very difficult pieces and worked on sight-reading. He would also have to be able to do things like find pitch with his voice, and other things that would have made my heart stop. Audition day came. He played Beethoven's Sonata No. 8 in C minor Op. 13 "Pathetique", an approximately 17 minute piece, and Chopin's Nocturne E Flat Major Op. 9 No. 2. I sat outside that performance room for what seemed like forever, but it was probably close to one and a half to two hours. Every now and then I'd catch a drift of piano music and my heart would jump hoping it was going off without a hitch but knowing that he'd never had a professional teacher, gone to college-run piano camps and such that it was a long shot. He came out looking rather shaken but with happy relief and sat beside me and we were asked to wait. Shortly after, the panel of four emerged with congratulations and welcomes to the Lock Haven Steinway School of Music. Shaking of hands went all around. Students just passing by stopped to congratulate him and say, "Alright man, welcome". It was amazing to me. He must have been floating.

Not long after that in 2010, John graduated high school with an accredited diploma with honors in history and music. He would turn eighteen two months later.

He had become friends with a wonderful girl, Erin some time before college. Not a girlfriend but a friend. A true, tell everything to, hang out whenever, sing-along-with the song playing even if you can't sing friend. It was just comfortable when they hung out and he enjoyed her company.

They had met through a mutual friend that John had met years before at camp and that Erin knew from high school. As Erin recalls, "We just hit it off right away, because we were both different and okay with that. Our taste in music was the same, our taste in everything matched. So we started to hang out more at my place and just sit on the porch and play guitar and eat pizza and all that stuff. Just close immediately, I don't even know how to explain it". Erin would become an incredible assest in the future.

They had been watching something and Erin said how lousy she had been feeling that week and how it made her feel better that he came up to talk and watch TV, and he said, "things can always be worse. Remember that". And she said, "How? My life is falling apart!!" And he said, "Hey man, at least your face isn't made of ants, because THAT would be terrible". She said they both laughed for probably ten minutes. After that when one of them was upset they would say that.

Lock Haven University (LHU)

And so began his pursuit of a music teaching degree at Lock Haven University. John moved into his dorm room near the end of August and met his roommate, Chris, a nice young man from New York. Classes began and all seemed well. He checked in with me most everyday on Social Media chat. He had his first cell phone. Daniel's gift to each of my kids for high school graduation has been to add them to his "friends and family" account, help them with their first phone and they only have to pay a small amount each month. Yes, none of my kids had a phone until after high school except Evy, who had one her senior year out of necessity and it was a pitiful hand-me-down phone. Anyway, I still had a prepaid flip phone and couldn't afford to text so we talked on Social Media.

He had classes each day, private piano instruction with his professor and then had to put in practice time on the piano as well. His dorm was right across the street from the music building so that was a convenience. We jokingly told him we were relieved that he didn't end up in one of the dorms at the top of the huge hill on campus because John was naturally clumsy, like his mom, and we said he would have spent more time falling down the hundreds of steps than he would have sitting in class. He had come home on a couple of weekends and he did seem a bit up tight but every first semester freshman does, right? It was a tough year for me too, tensions were high at home and as always John and I were connected. Even as a little kid he would come into my room and climb up beside me and hug me and say, "it's okay Mama, I love you, you're a good Mama." He just knew when that was needed.

Sometimes he'd message me and ask if I was okay that day somehow knowing I really wasn't. I always had a concern deep down about how he would do. I'm not exactly sure why or how. It's not that I didn't think he was smart enough or had the ability, Just knew something. It didn't sit well. One night as I was on the computer he popped on and asked, "Mom, how bad does depression get?" My heart sank. I got my thoughts together and remembered any psych training I had and personal experiences and asked non-leading questions so I didn't put words in his mouth. I started out by asking why he was asking hoping maybe he was worried about his roommate or a friend. No, it was about him. He began by telling me that he felt really down and didn't want to do stuff and was overwhelmed. I tried to talk about how the beginning of something new and difficult and different can have that effect. We talked about trying to get better organized, make a schedule and stick to it. Think about what he was eating, all the things you should suggest.

I really wish I had written down in detail everything he said so I could look back on it but I just needed to listen at the time and I think it would just break my heart even more now ruminating over what else I could have done in the beginning.

I can hear his voice in my mind even now trying to express himself, connecting instantly and feeling a rock in my stomach. When you know your child, like most parents do, you know it's not a normal wrong. What he said to me took me back to my own feelings of twisted confusion and so I continued to ask him to explain. He said it had been going on for a while. He felt lethargic but anxious, his thoughts couldn't be kept straight and he was exhausted but couldn't sleep, at all. He was lucky to doze for two hours each night. He didn't want to shower and he didn't care. His friends would try to get him to come to the dining hall, even come to his door and prod him but he wouldn't go, couldn't, even when he tried. He said he got angry at the drop of a hat but not at anything in particular and then would turn around and feel so badly about it, soon after he'd be in tears.

Fortunately several of the friends at school with him he had known awhile and didn't abandon him during this first rough spot. They cared a great deal about his wellbeing and really tried to help. He was beside himself, panicked that he would fail at what he was doing and let everyone down. I told him to keep holding on and try his best to stay on track for the rest of the week and I'd see about getting him an appointment to see somebody. He said he would try and would check in as often as he could.

I started calling the next morning to find out what I could about getting him in to see someone. We were still dealing with the county system because of our insurance and it tends to be overburdened and sometimes slow. I spoke to them on the phone to set up an intake appointment. They let me do that for him but everything else had to be taken care of by him since he was over eighteen unless he signed forms allowing me to be a part of everything due to HIPPA laws. He did that at the first appointment because he wanted me to be aware and to make things easier too. It was almost a month before he could get in for the appointment and we talked frequently about everything. He kept track of how he was feeling as I had asked him to. He continued not to be able to sleep, his thoughts raced, he was extremely anxious and nervous, yet he would spend hours "inside his own head". The best way we found to explain it some days was it was like going out and doing your day without ever leaving your bed in your mind. He still did his best to go to classes and lessons. He put on an incredible face to the public and in the end some people never even knew he had been ill.

He'd come home weekends and we'd talk and I'd explain that I knew how he felt, really and at that time I told him more details about me and he was relieved that I really did understand what he was talking about. He had know for years that Mom had something going on but now it made more sense and it also clicked for him why we were so much alike. I vowed to him that I would never give up on him and do what I could to help him. He was my son and I loved him no matter what.

With everything he had been going through, his behaviors and symptoms and even going through psychological checklists available he was really falling on the bipolar illness chart. Unfortunately "just" being his mother for 18 years and living with the disease myself apparently counts zero percent towards input for a diagnosis. My trusted psychiatrist had retired many years before or I think we would have had a much better chance of quick and more successful treatment of John but that wasn't the case.

He was examined and they determined it was stress and depression. They prescribed an anti-depressant. Through years of research I became very alarmed because it can be dangerous to prescribe an anti-depressant to a bipolar patient without also adding a mood stabilizer as it can often times cause them to spiral downward and they can become suicidal or throw them into a manic or hypomanic state. I tried to discuss this with them, explaining his and my background, history and my reasoning but I was brushed off and told they refuse to diagnose a patient with bipolar without first seeing proof of a manic episode. (This is not always the case) Some people with bipolar may not have a manic episode for years or have a manic episode of "textbook intensity" that would warrant some therapists to see it as such. In the appendices I have included several bipolar informational inserts from relevant and qualified medical organizations to help people understand the wide range of symptoms of depression and mania associated with this debilitating and sometimes confusing disease.

He began taking the medication and returned to school. It was late October by now and he felt a bit of an upswing in his mood and struggled on in his studies but continued to feel about he same overall. He looked poorly, with "blue face", we used to say the he didn't get dark circles under his eyes but got blue around his eyes and a bluish tinge to him. He would have his up days and was still everyone's friend and always had time to meet someone new or help out a buddy. I think his personality was just the sort that helped him push back the dark so he could focus on others and not get swept under as long as possible. He played his music to keep his head above water and was doing his best. When he came home he often would flop on to the floor in what we called the schoolroom and just lay there for the longest time and the kids and I would congregate around him like the old school days and laugh and joke. There were times his dad would get upset about his behavior and yell at him to snap out of it and shape up. He often felt I was coddling him and that John was being a wimp and trying to get out of things and making excuses. It probably didn't help that at times John was his old self laughing and being a cut up and then crashed emotionally. It was another wedge being driven between him and his dad and his dad and me.

He kept a daily log of moods during the time period leading up to his first appointment. Some of the entries give insight to how his mind was working and makes you wonder how his body was still getting him through the days. He had also been encouraged to cut back on sugar intake, keep track of what caused the most emotional discomfort and difficulty and to find things or places that help him relax. He was also to go back in his mind to when he was little to think of things and time periods that set him off and to identify times that he had done self-injury. He had done cutting. (The following are excerpts)

Oct. 6: *Wednesday, Afternoon/night- Frustrated, incapable of playing instruments, irritable, energetic, feeling like I'm failing at little things. Sad.*

Oct. 8: Friday- Irritable, tired, relaxed, sad at times-but was upset and cried on the floor when Mom and Dad fought. Not as lethargic as the last two days but still not feeling motivated to do anything.

Oct. 9: *Saturday- Overall feeling of not having the urge to do anything, still relatively down and sad, lethargic but it went away around 4. Not as tired today. Insomnia- I was up until 2 am on Sunday, slightly irritable, displeased with physical appearance.*

Oct.12: *Not feeling or seeing any point to this day. Just want to lie on my bed and cry. Sick to my stomach. Struggling to play any music, irritable, just want to cry about anything that upsets me or frustrates me. Sudden upturn in the day, have my energy back, Still kinda wish that today would hurry up, excited that Emily (girlfriend at the time) got accepted to Lock Haven.*

Oct. 14: *Feeling strangely good and upbeat, getting my energy back. Feeling a little more emotionally stable, much more alert and attentive, feeling happier overall, actually feeling like doing something productive and motivated to do it. Having a feeling tonight is going to be a really long night because I got really warm all of a sudden and a huge burst of energy from out of nowhere hit me and I feel like I could do anything. Feeling happy still and like everything is getting better.*

Oct. 17: *Down, insomnia, super stressed out, scared of possible outcomes if I* *fail my two midterms tomorrow. Feeling crappy about myself, want to make everyone go away that doesn't understand me, in an "I don't give a fuck" mood towards most people.*

Oct. 18: *Sad, down, no sleep the night before, woke up in a panic attack and cold sweat. Insomnia, feeling down about myself in school, feeling alright about my playing though. Happy I have Emily and Mom to get me through the days.*

Oct. 20: *So worn out. Feeling like someone sneaks into my room every night and steals my energy as I sleep. Which is still only 2 hours every night. Feeling it's only there to kill time till the next day. Only ate breakfast and beans and peanut butter at like 10. Not feeling hungry at all. Irritable, sick of the damn people in my dorm making noise, pissed with the sarcasm from people, which I really don't mind usually. I look like crap, no motivation to shave or really get my hair done. No motivation for a lot of things, just want to lie in bed. Feeling like college is kind of a mistake. I'm way too inferior to everyone here, I don't want to hang out or talk to anyone 'cause they are all a bunch of assholes, or annoy me, but I still need to put on a happy face and not lead on that I really don't want to talk to them. There are a few exceptions though, I don't feel like that towards Mom or Emily, they're trying to help a ton. Randomly crying over simple little things and feeling like anything sets me off. Honestly I wouldn't mind not waking up tomorrow. I know I'm only gonna get two freaking hours of sleep again and I'll still have to get out of bed and have another day to drudge through.*

Oct. 22: *Actually got a good night's sleep for once.*

Oct. 25: *Kind of an up and down day. Felt like I can't really get a good grasp on playing the piano. Feeling kinda sick, have a temperature of 100.2F and randomly sweaty with a huge headache at around three pm onwards. Felt happy most of the day except when I felt like crap about myself. God, I don't know why suicidal thoughts are jumping into my head, like different ways I could go out, but I love life.*

Oct. 27: *Awful morning, slept in...Freaking out when I remember something I forgot and thinking I'm a complete idiot. Happy today about most things... Not seeing myself as super important, I really want to help everyone out.*

His handwriting got very erratic when he was struggling and sometimes got hard to decipher.

Oct. 28: *Good day until I had to go fuck things up. He had had okay classes, and his intake call for psych appointment, during which he says he, "was upbeat but nervous and thought I was going to cry a few times". He then had to wait for his first "in person" appointment. But because of worrying about a paper apparently he got mad at Emily and made her cry. I can make out, I feel absolutely awful. I know I hurt her. I hate it. I always do. Sometimes I think I'll just only hurt her just once more and no more by killing myself. That would solve everything, my stress, my lack of sleep, family problems…I can't though, I promised her I wouldn't and I can't do that. I wish I was different, not a screw up maybe then I'd be good, but no, I'm just John the idiot. Lots of suicidal thoughts lately when I'm down.*

Nov. 3: *Bad Day… Thought of ending everything today in the slowest, most painful way I could think of 'cause I've hurt a ton of people so much and they've seen me try to change and fail. I thought of crashing my car into a pillar of an overpass, or drown myself, or starve myself for weeks on end 'cause I'd wither away and constantly be in pain so I'd know how I've made everyone else feel throughout my life. I'd be a lot better off…I feel like I'm forcing laughter and smiles.*

Everyday gets worse. I see no point in waking up or going to class. I feel like I'm a moron. Everyday I struggle getting out of bed and staying awake in class. I want to hurl myself down a flight of stairs just to not have to face the fucking day. I've been so emotional and crying so much, single words that aren't even emotional set me off, commercials make me cry. I look like crap. I look so ugly and fat. No energy for the last few days, just lethargic. Not very irritable just don't feel like talking to people. OCD about certain things like my rug but letting other things go to crap.

That is the last formal entry in that notebook.

Between November and Christmas break he got worse, more depressed and discouraged talking about how hugely he was failing, what a disappointment he was. No amount of encouragement helped. It's hard to believe he continued to go to class at all and passed them. He looked like the walking dead because he didn't sleep. His cousin of the same age was quite ill at the same time and waiting for a diagnosis of what turned out to be Hashimoto's disease and she was doing nothing but sleep and he used to say he wanted to trade Kristen some of his wakefulness for some of her sleep.

Break came and although tensions were high at home he was at least getting a bit of time off of school. Spring semester was to start up again in mid January and right before it did John went into what the doctor would finally accept as a manic episode. He was exhilarated and non-stop. He was full of ideas and just music, music, music. He was very agitated and hyper and quick to get irritated but not angry, very emotional. After reading the entries in his log it sounds as though he may have been in a mixed state at times in the beginning. They got him into the office and decided to put him on lithium, which is a very commonly used and traditional medication for bipolar. In my mind I had wished they had put him on the combination that had been successful for me for so many years, especially since we were so alike.

I still do wonder how things would have gone for him had they gone this route from the beginning or at least tried it along the way. But, this is the route they wanted to go. He started the lithium the second, third and fourth day of the new semester. It went very badly. He was most likely allergic to it. He ended up coming home. He broke out in a terrible sweat, was dizzy, laid on the floor writhing with stomach pain, vomited and just felt generally horrible. When I called the office they didn't seem overly concerned. They explained he might just need to get used to the medication. I forcefully re-explained his symptoms and they said maybe he should stop the lithium. I asked what they would try next and when should I pick it up at the pharmacy. They said that they would reevaluate when they saw him in a month. I was furious. He was devastated. He had finally felt relieved that they diagnosed him and now he felt they were brushing him off. He just felt defeated, as did I.

So semester number two is already off to a bad start but he pushes on. By this time he has gained significant weight, just as I had from medication. This is not helping his depression in the least. He is finally prescribed another medication, to add to the anti-depressant and this finally starts to cause some improvement. He learns that it may take some trial and error before a good combination is found. During the five years he was treated for bipolar he was prescribed the following medications and more. I don't have a complete list of all the things he tried but I wish now that I did.

Lamictal	celexa	klonopin	depakote
abilify	lorazapam	diazepam	zypreza
atarax	wellbutrin		

He got through his second semester with passing grades, not spectacular but he wasn't on academic probation either. He came home for the summer.

John was afraid of heights and decided to try to conquer that fear by taking a job that summer working with a childhood friend doing exterior house painting. Now, remember we live in an area chock full of beautiful, large, tall, Victorian homes. He worked really hard that summer and usually was gone ten or eleven hours a day. He came home covered in paint. His cutoff camo shorts could pretty much stand up alone they were so think with dried paint. He told us how he would be harnessed in and tied off on third story jobs. He still didn't like being up high but he did it. I think the hard physical work was a good thing for him and he liked being constantly moving even though he was exhausted.

He opened a checking account that summer and in the car he told me he thought it would be best for him not to get the ATM card with the account because he knew that impulse buying was a big weakness of his he knew that the harder it was for him to get to his money the better that would be. I agreed and complimented him on his foresight.

He was taking his medication but was extremely dissatisfied with the weight gain so they had changed it to something else and during the summer with that change and the exercise he began to lose some weight. Fall semester 2011 came and it was time to move back to the dorm and he was quite upbeat. He was going to room with Brad, the band's drummer that he had known since high school, and was happy that his then girlfriend, Emily would be at school too. He had signed up to be part of the LHU jazz small and large ensembles, which meant he would get formal instruction on the bass and get to perform with the group. He was still with the same piano profession for lessons, which he was thrilled with, as he liked Dr. Curtin both as an instructor and as a person. He said there was something about him. His sister later took a music class with him when she was a student at LHU just to get the experience. She liked him too.

I was unable to be there to help him move in, one of our favorite things. He liked to let me make his bed, like old camp days. My dad had become suddenly quite ill with Guillain Barre Syndrome and I had been in Pittsburgh for a while with him. John had volunteered to be a "mover and Shaker" that year which meant he went back a couple of before the other arriving students and then when they did arrive he and the others met the cars outside the dorms with carts and manpower to unload vehicles all day and quickly move everybody into to their rooms fast and efficiently.

The semester started out well. Then he, like many others with bipolar or depression began feeling better because the meds were working and stopped taking them because he thought he didn't need them anymore. He began to relapse into the depression again. I didn't know how bad until I got a call from his girlfriend who said she had gone to his room for something and discovered he was just about to go to the river to end it. He said he had planned to fill his backpack with rocks once he reached the dyke near campus and jump in the Susquehanna River and let himself sink to the bottom. She was taking him to the hospital as instructed by the clinic where they had gone. I headed out immediately. This was my first step into the world of hospital mental health. Unfortunately it would not be my last.

Upon check in at the hospital ER it was just John and myself. You have no idea how hard it is to sit quietly and calm-faced as you listen to your son tell the intake nurse what his suicide plan was. You listen and hear things you never wanted to hear. You learn that he has been seeking out Vicatin since after he had his wisdom teeth out and snagging extras when his brother had his teeth out. You don't think about that stuff in your cupboard, you don't think you have to. Now I have every thing that seems remotely addictive in a safe because the cats might want it! You learn he tried pot when he was twelve and still smokes sometimes and he had been a cutter. You want to jump out of that stupid plastic chair and hug him and cry with him but you have to sit there and be, well, just be.

You wait for them to print off that little paper wristband and take you to another waiting place and when you get there he tells you he's sorry you had to hear all that, and you reply that it's ok and that he needs to tell them everything so that they can help him. Meanwhile you feel like a failure because you are the mom and you want to fix it. You also feel stupid and naive that it happened right in front of you, but it's pretty easy to hide really. He wasn't smoking at home and missing pills were easily overlooked and he didn't act or look like the "druggies " they show on TV and in the movies, you know?

Next, a million people come in and get histories and they tell you who they are and you forget who they are five seconds after they leave. You just want someone to explain how this works and what they meant when they say we are waiting to see if there is a bed for him, as if he'd get a sleeping bag instead. Eventually someone explains it all and it makes sense. They explain that He will be upstairs in the Behavioral Health Unit and it is strictly monitored. You have to be buzzed in and visitors can only come at two pre-set visiting times a day for two-hour periods.

You have to lock all your belongings, like purses, phones, coats, and bags in a locker outside the unit and be let in. He would list only the people he wants to visit to be put on the list. I was given a number to the nurses station, which I could call at anytime time to get an update on him. He had to take laces out of his shoes and drawstrings out of pants or hoodies. There were group and individual meetings for him to attend daily. They would work on getting his meds adjusted, set up therapist appointments and aftercare and give a medical excuse to the college. There were activities like puzzles and crafts if he wanted to do them and books and a TV room that was monitored. A family meeting was held a couple days prior to his leaving to set goals together. The minimum stay was five days (recommended). He had voluntarily checked in and could check himself out if he had wanted to.

On a side note, when you are done with a jigsaw puzzle donate them to your local behavioral health facility. They would probably love a new batch to put out. One thing I always do at Christmas is go to a discount store near me and pick out 3 or 4 new puzzles and put them in a gift bag. I head to the hospital and take them directly to the unit. Some of the staff are the same and remember John. I let them know how much I appreciated all they did to help my son and for the work they do, then give them the bag. It is always emotional but worth it.

You could see his nervousness and a bit of relief as we rode up the elevator together. He asked for a few things from home, which were allowed. One was his Teddy. We were to be heading to North Carolina for Nationals, a yearly kayak competition Evy and Ethan had been training for, I didn't want to leave John in this situation and neither did Evy and Ethan but this was once a year and national rankings were at stake for them. My mom offered to drive in from Pittsburgh and take the kids down for me and let them walk her through the details once there. This time we would be staying in a hotel so that was a bonus. So we took her up on it. By the time she got to town the next day John had convinced me that he wanted me to go with Evy and Ethan. He reasoned that I could only come a couple hours each day anyway and he had Emily and his dad could come. Fortunately some friends stopped up too. So reluctantly I agreed.

To add to a bad situation while John was dealing with his first rock bottom his dad had to break the news to him that his cat, Otis, the one who was his best buddy, one of three we had raised on bottles, had been hit by a car and died between Friday night and Saturday morning. This was one more thing for him to try to manage. It was a blow to all of us and was hard to take on top of everything else but even worse for him.

We, the kids, Mom and I were only gone a few days and we were home in time for a few visits to the hospital and for his dad and me to attend the family meeting. It went pretty well. They explained that he had been given some coping skills, initial appointments with a therapist local to the university, what his new meds would be etc. He was able to voice, uninterrupted, his concerns and hopes for recovery at home and his desire to be understood by everyone there. The doctor and therapist did their best to explain to all of us that his illness is not one that just goes away, that he would need to treat it for a lifetime and that he would need the whole family's support. I hoped this would be a positive point on which to build. He was released a day or two later after eight days.

By this time his good friend Erin had started college and she recalls,
"He really started to tell me he was struggling when we were in college. It was my first year there, so it would have been his second. He was rooming with Brad at the time. It came on slowly, but I noticed that he was looking more tired and more withdrawn, but when it was just he and I it was just like old times. He would tell me every now and again that he was feeling 'low' or 'numb' but he didn't start really vocalizing the severity of things until I pushed and asked. I could usually tell when he was really up, and try to catch the down before it happened; sometimes I couldn't because it would happen so quickly. He would text me and say like, 'I just need to talk' or 'do you work tonight, can we have a late night music and cigarette night?' And I knew that he needed to get some stuff off his chest. A way that I figured out was to listen to the music he was listening to at the time. He would change what he listened to depending on what he was really feeling and that was always a give away to me that there was something else going on. He opened up most to me honestly in his notes. (He wrote letters and notes-he liked hand written correspondence) I think it was easier for him to write stuff down than to say it. He would tell me things in a letter and then I would talk to him about it and he wouldn't want to talk about it, but would respond to what I said, in another letter. I think it was just easier for him."

It's hard to remember sometimes the order and progression of things at this point. I do remember in that year's Christmas picture he was heavy and he hated the photo so he had to have gained again on the meds, which concerned me that he would quit them considering how low his self-image could drop. John's episodes seemed to stabilize for a while. He kept up with classes and being a member of both the large and small Jazz ensembles for LHU. We attended the winter performance and it was fantastic. They had a guest performer there, a gentleman who played many years with Tito Puente. It was thrilling to watch him up there in his element.

January of 2011 came and he began a new semester his second rooming with Brad. During discussions with Brad he described this year with John as a very emotional one. He would often find John in bed for what seemed to be days. He saw his extreme mood swings and experienced the best and worst of John. Fortunately for John and for us he didn't give up on him. Brad knew John had been doing some cutting at the time, "it helped release some of the pain", is how he explained it. He was a dedicated friend and did his best to coax him to eat and to be social, keep attending class and encouraged him as best he could. Having the band was a huge help. Brad helped John through relationship difficulties, John was there for Brad as well but it was a tumultuous time. When John was hospitalized Brad visited and was supportive. He didn't cut and run like some friends would have when mental illness came into play.

Fall of 2012 John and Ethan were ready to begin LHU together as roommates by choice. After some difficulties and debate about finances both boys were going to be living on campus and they wanted to be roommates. They were comfortable with each other, knew each other's quirks. After all, they had been rooming together all their lives and Ethan felt there was no way he could get a roommate messier than his brother so he might as well just keep living with him! The Semester started out pretty well, it seemed. He was enjoying introducing his brother to the campus and people he already knew and the two of them grew even closer. The band was doing well too. His girlfriend, Kayla was very good for him and also got along with Ethan and their friends. She really seemed to understand the person he was and was patient with him. She was, and still is an amazing woman. They had a special book that they wrote back and forth in to each other and I think this helped him express himself in a safe environment. Kayla never judged him, nor did she let him get away with stupid crap either as Erin has expressed to me.

John had a beautiful way of looking at the world and wished everyone else to see it that way too. I think he wanted everyone to hold on to life as hard as he was trying to...

"Everything was beautiful and nothing hurt", this quote from Kurt Vonnegut's novel Slaughterhouse Five, a favorite book of John's, is written in Sharpie on his laptop case.

So much of the person he was seemed to focus on how he made others feel and how he could touch their hearts, but he did it with ease. I don't think he got up each morning, thinking, "I have to make sure I am nice to at least three people". It was just who he was.

Ethan called me one September evening saying that his brother was not well, that he was "like he had been when he went to the hospital before". I asked if he knew if he had taken anything or was drinking. He did the best he could to explain but it was easy to tell that he wasn't sure how to handle it and he suddenly felt like his brother's keeper. I quickly realized I didn't need two going down so I gave Ethan the "Can Help" (crisis hotline) number and told him to call since LHU didn't have 24 hour on campus help lines at the time being a very small school. He got off the phone after saying he'd call back. I paced and waited, feeling anxious for the both of them. He called back and said they were going to have the campus police transport John to our hospital and Ethan would stay behind. By the time I got to the hospital the campus police had gone but John was calm and said they were very nice to him and the staff said those who transported him said John had been nothing but cooperative and positive with them.

It was during this stay, his third hospitalization, he would end up being hospitalized five times in total, that John knew his journey was going to be a long one and that stress was something that was a huge trigger for both manic and depressive episodes. After meeting with doctors it was discovered that he had been having psychotic episodes and may have experienced them before but may not have been able to explain them, may not have wanted to or may not have been asked detailed enough questions about symptoms.

Anyway that was in the mix now so his bipolar I was of the severe type now for sure. We still found ways to laugh and be upbeat on visits. As mentioned before you had to lock up everything in little lockers before you go into the unit. They have keys like bus station lockers that you take with you. I picked locker 15 as it's my favorite number but when we (Evy, Ethan and I) got to the room Kayla and their good friend Kenny were already there and in the silliness talking about lockers I held up my key and mistakenly said, "I always pick 15, it's my favorite color". It's been a joke ever since.

John made the decision to withdraw from college at that time and not make any decisions about what to do from there too quickly. He was given new prescriptions including one for anxiety. The following week he and I went to the appropriate offices at LHU and did the paperwork for medical withdraw and the women in the office were exceptionally nice and helped us every step of the way. He did lose a portion of his tuition and room and board but not 100%. After that he and his brother and I packed up his things and loaded up the van and left Ethan in what looked like a very lonely and empty room.

Carol Fayman
August 4 at 6:49 am

My tribute to you my sweet friend, I'm sorry we drifted apart after I left for school. It's so unfortunate that I didn't say these things to you before. And I know now that you're gone my words Mean so little, that it's even foolish on social media. At first I didn't believe it. You were oh so loved by so many, if there could be one more day you would know it. I'll truly miss you John. I'll always remember our crazy nights, costume parties, serious talks. And as I was looking through memories I don't know why I don't have any real photos or selfies of us, but I'll never forget all the laughs and awkward moments. Maybe someday I'll see you again. John Van Horn.

Chloe Noelle > John Van Horn
August 29 at 6:32 pm

"I mean, there's always the sunset and sunrise to look forward to."
A little phrase John Van Horn came up with for me one day. After that, it kind of stuck. It was one of our "things".
Anytime I was sad he would say that mo me in his little happy-go-lucky way.
And I'd smile.
I miss you so much Johnny.
It hurts.
Every day.
I'd give anything to see your face once more time and hear you say that.
Look into your little twinkling eyes and see that phrase form on your lips.
I'll never forget you Johnny.
You have a special piece of my heart that will belong to you forever.
Love you Johnny.

Kayla Miller
October 26

"Every day is a new day to be something more. Everyday I have the power to decide who I am. I have the power to be who I need to be. My future is as bright as I make it to be. We are all so important and that's just the greatest thing I think."
A little something John Van Horn wrote for me in our "book of letters."

Cassie Nicole
August 5 at 8:43 am

Its crazy how life spins in directions you never expect, There was one person who gave me the life today. Shown us that college wasn't scary and Lock Haven was a giant family... Made us the way we are. The first year in college we depended on each other while life was hitting us hard in all ways possible we all found each other to love and support. I never want to let go of the friends that I made and carried on that year. Thanks guys forever. Rip John.......

Carol Fayman
August 8 at 12:59 pm

This is for you John Van Horn. When someone passes away you say they were a good person, but in this case you would be insane to say he wasn't. To say John was a good person in an understatement. Willing to do anything to help a friend, John was selfless, kind hearted, and always turns your bad day into a good one simply by his smile. Even in death he helped others, saving four lives by donating his organs. Your time here is finished but you'll live forever in my memories sweet friend.

Sharon Hicks

I'll also never forget that time he walked into Big Lots with and eight inch Mohawk...but I didn't recognize him until I saw his pink sneakers, lol. He later became employed there, them never knowing he was the kid with the Mohawk, lol. I sure am going to miss him. I just saw him on Wednesday night at Sheetz...He didn't want to share my fries.

Not only was this a big change for John it was a heavy blow to Ethan. He was now on his own at college for the first time (it's still October) with no roommate with an extremely heavy class load and certainly concerned about his brother. Ethan was on a medical field track at the time and was carrying anatomy and physiology and biology, which had total lab time of five hours a week along with his other courses. Considering what a quiet person he is I was concerned about his being so alone. He did fill out paperwork to get a roommate for the spring semester. With his experience and exposure to a variety of cultures through kayaking he checked the box saying he was willing to have an international student roommate and was paired with a really nice young man from Korea in January and he enjoyed that very much.

I look back now and fear that Ethan may have gotten lost in the fray at this time. So much energy is being spent on the issues at hand one tends to think the guy with fewer problems will keep on going. Evy was still living at home so interaction with her was easy. Ethan was pretty quiet to start. He and I had never been two that texted or chatted on Social Media together before this so all of this must have impacted him far more than anyone ever knew.

Once John got back home it was a bit difficult getting everyone on the same page.

He was trying to normalize. I wasn't sure how long to give him to settle in, his sister was glad to have him around again during her school day and his dad wanted him out finding a job in a week, so calculate that dynamic.

So John's time as a college student at LHU had ended, leaving both good and bad experiences behind but he most certainly met wonderful people there and will be remembered by those he left behind.

Because of the amount of time they had spent together on individual and classroom instruction and because of how highly John had spoken of Dr.Curtin I felt I needed to get a hold of him concerning John's death. In my email I thanked him for the care and time he had taken with my son and made sure he knew of John's gratitude and admiration. This is the response I received:

Dear Michelle,
I don't know what to say except that I am so terribly sorry. I appreciated your thanks but it was entirely my pleasure to know John. He was so easy to be around, with that beautiful smiling face of his. Whatever help I gave him, whatever I was able to teach him, I was just doing my job. But being the way he was, he made that job easy for me, because was a truly special guy. His gentle spirit, his positive attitude—despite the troubles he was going

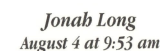

Jonah Long
August 4 at 9:53 am

It saddens me to hear that another friend has passed away. John Van Horn you were one of the first friends I made up at Lock Haven, and you were truly always there for everyone. You helped to teach me to always be myself, no matter what anyone else thought. I'm gonna miss you my friend. You truly were one of a kind.

Who would've thought we'd all become friends at a bench between dorm buildings. Just sitting there listening to him play his guitar is something I'll never forget.

Cora Talarigo
August 4 at 8:40 am

RIP John Van Horn. You were loved by many and will be missed by many. I know we weren't close, but I know you were a wonderful friend to many. I always enjoyed running into you when I was out and about and talking to you whether it be for a few seconds or much longer. I also want to say a prayer for all of the friends and family that are experiencing this loss.

Cassie Nicole
August 8 at 2pm

Went to John Van Horn's favorite spot before we left Lock Haven. Sent candles down the river from the dyke in honor of someone who enjoyed the simple things in life.

Cassie Nicole > John Van Horn
September 29

John it's raining in LHU but I'm waiting for the clouds to set on the mountains. I knew you always liked the way that looked!!!! Miss you forever buddy! !!! #RIP through behind the scenes, which no one would have known about from casual acquaintance—made him stand out from the thousands of students I have dealt with over the years. In this job, over time, one can become weary and jaded sometimes about college students—it has probably always been so. But all it takes is one John Van Horn to wipe all those feelings away. I am so sad that we have lost him. I am touched that you took the time in your grief to contact me, but I hope that you will understand when I say that I wish I didn't know. I'm sure I would have found out eventually anyway, but I wish I could think of his smiling face still being out there somewhere. The world is a lesser place without him.

Please accept my deepest condolences to you and your family.
David Curtin

I had the opportunity to spend several hours talking with Dr. Curtin a few years after John's death and we spoke about many things. Near the end of the conversation he said he wasn't sure if he had been able to give me any good information for this book but he felt that possibly what stood out about John most was that as he looks at the youth of today he sees so many of them just going through their lives "existing", going through the motions of the day. He sees them being on devices, not interacting with each other before or after class. He sees little motivation for them desiring to improve themselves. If they receive a C or D grade they just accept it as so and move on without any want to improve or even an interest as to why they received that grade.

They almost seem numb. He found John to be different in that he was excited about things. He interacted with others and worked to improve himself and wanted more. He felt there was something different, an enthusiasm that had been absent and it encouraged him. He told me that Evelyn had given him two pictures of John while she was he student and he keeps them both placed where he can see them. One is in his office so he can see John's bright smile and the other is near his piano. It warms my heart to know that he is still reaching people, encouraging people and making a difference here. It is still an honor to call him my son and it makes me want to continue to improve myself.

The Educational Gap of Oct. 2012 - Aug. 2014

After leaving LHU John had to figure out what he wanted to do. He got a job at the Dollar General store in town and really enjoyed the interaction with people. Being such a social guy he got along well with everybody. In December of 2012 one of John's childhood dreams came true. He purchased a 1981 Mazda RX7, a car he had loved since he was about 8. It was nearby his Grammy and her husband's house outside of Pittsburgh. A deal was made and he and his dad drove out and brought it back on a snowy afternoon. A picture of him standing beside it in our driveway can be found among the photos.

He spent many happy hours tooling around in 'lil Blue as he named her. He also enrolled in and completed a phlebotomy (blood drawing) course in the spring of 2013. He did pretty well but decided against doing it long-term. He stayed with the dollar store until not long before he began the next educational chapter of his life.

The Central Pennsylvania Institute of Science & Technology (CPI)

The Central Pennsylvania Institute of Science and Technology, CPI is where John got another new start. As a matter of fact it's where the four of us got another new start. In the fall of 2014 John, Ethan, Evelyn and I all went to school together. Sounds crazy, but we did. At CPI, there are nineteen programs, most of which combine high school students from three local high schools with adult students. It's an accredited post secondary school so we were able to use grant money and Evelyn was still a senior and although homeschooled was a resident of one of the sending school districts and could attend at no cost. Evelyn studied Collision Repair. Ethan studied Horticulture/Landscaping. I took Structural Welding and John took Precision Machining.

It was really fun being together. We actually had fun buying all of our steel-toed boots together and things like that. Ethan was the only one of us whose classroom wasn't in the same wing of the building. Everyone got a kick out of the "four Van Horn's" at school. As always John wasn't embarrassed to have me around and it was great because the welding shop and machine shop each had their own shop but shared a mutual shop together so often times we'd see each other and he'd call out "hi mom", and point out to classmates, "that's my mom, in welding". He'd tell me he was proud of me. His instructor, Ben, told me he always enjoyed their conversations and

Ethan W Amy > John Van Horn
August 4 at 10:25 am

I'm at a loss for words. I'm so glad I got to meet you and get to know you and share a love of music with ya over the last few years. You were one of the nicest and funniest guys I've ever met. You will truly be missed, Rest easy man.

Tanner Light
August 4 at 10:52 am

Still can't even begin to fathom that you're no longer with us John Van Horn. I know we just started talking in school but you were such a kind hearted individual and you were always so happy. Your time with us was short, but you brightened the lives of so many people. Personally, I'm so glad I got to know you and listen to you play the guitar. Although I won't be able to hear you play anymore, don't quit playing up in heaven. Watch over your friends and family and keep that beautiful smile on your face. Rest easy brother.

Johnny Rossman > John Van Horn
August 4 at 9:57 am

Rest in Peace, brother, and play the Angels a tune for us.

Mason Aber > John Van Horn
August 4 at 12:26 am

"The great thing about life; Nobody makes it out alive, so don't take it too seriously." You could really make me laugh man, you made coming to school all the more worth it. I always got a kick out of that little blue demon of yours too.

Looking back on our conversations, one that comes to mind right now is one we had about how much we both hated funerals because of how sad they can be. We agreed you should instead celebrate a person's life and remember the good times you had with them.

I might have only known you for a short time but I still consider you a good friend and one I won't soon forget. Rest easy John,

Derik Cruz
August 4 at 12:09pm

Really sad to hear about the passing to an LHU friend, John Van Horn. It was an honor to learn about, and play music together in our short time as classmates. A great musician, a better dude. Peace, friend...

Jeff Lord
August 4 at 9:00 am

Saddened to learn of the passing of former coworker John Van Horn. You were one of the few coworkers that could talk guitars, and music, and actually knew what good music was! I am still in disbelief. I just saw you a few weeks ago. RIP John. Condolences to Ethan and the rest of the family.

Mike Winger > John Van Horn
August 4 at 10:52 am

Met him at a party once then started working with him and let me say it was always a fun shift when he was working. Never seemed stressed and always looking to help anyone out. I can't believe this.

Kevin Keen > John Van Horn
August 4 at 1:21 am

There is so much I could say about someone that was so well liked and so well loved. One of the best and most genuine people I have ever met.
You never pulled any punches and you never failed to make anyone laugh. I will miss you dearly, my friend.

Nancy Jo Schneider-Moore
August 4 at 3:33 pm

When I was at work yesterday, I looked at the schedule to see it I would be working with John Van Horn, and I was so excited to see we would be working together on Saturday. I hadn't seen him for about 3 weeks. It hurts to know that my silly young "school son", as we called him, will never be silly around me again. Rest in peace young man, and don't trip over the clouds up there.

he found John interesting. He was also amused by John's whimsical spirit. When his class would come into our shared shop he'd always jokingly remind John not to look directly at the bright light from the welding and John would say he wanted to because it was so pretty, and then laugh.

For the first few months of class it was hard for the both of us to be confident in ourselves. I had an especially difficult time accepting that anything that I did was going to be good enough. My instructor, who was outstanding, would look and my work and tell me that three-fourths of my weld bead was great and show me where the other fourth needed to improve because of porosity or an inclusion and I would automatically hear, "the whole things sucks, you can't do anything right". I focused only on the mistake because that's how I had been programmed for so long. I could encourage anyone else, but not myself. John must have been doing the same thing because on many days on lunch break he'd come over to my shop when no one was around and lean on me for a hug and cry and tell me he couldn't do it (school) and say, "when am I going to get him out of my head?" I could only respond by telling him I didn't know but we had to try and if nothing else we had to succeed to prove him wrong.

John just being goofy John in a mirror at the store where his sister was working. A favorite shot of many people. When the store closed the management allowed Evy to keep the mirror.

Mason Aber
August 6 at 5:16 pm

Typically I don't do throwback Thursdays but this is different. Here's a great picture of John being John, posing with the freshly stretched tractor. Covered in dirt like always, and I'm sure he was doing his goofy laugh when this was taken. You were called home too early, but I like to think that things are little more exciting with you up there.

Alex Steel
August 4 at 9:55 pm

I don't even know what to say. John was one of the greatest bassists that I know. Every time he played I was in awe. I remember being at his house and he was showing me what he knew on piano and it made me weep it was so freaken good. I could listen to him play acoustic guitar for hours and most of the time when we were in a band together that's what we did. He knew every song I loved and could play it even better. I just wish I had more time so we could have played together more. Rest in peace John Van Horn. I remember singing with him while he played this song and it will always remind me of him.
Linoleum-Streetlight Manifesto

RussDauberman
August 4 at 10:03 am

I can't believe I'm posting this right now...but I met this dude@ painintheeasttronaut about a year ago and he was one of the most genuine and unique people I've ever been graced with getting to know, not to mention one of the most incredible musicians with whom I've ever had the honor of sharing the stage. Though our friendship was just beginning to bloom, I surely considered you a friend and could more importantly see what a great friend/ person you were to so many people. You are a true legend, a true punk, and an inspiration to all. I remember when you posted the picture on the right I laughed so fucking hard. It truly embodies your hilarious sense of humor and ability to live life the way more people ought to do. You will be greatly missed and I won't forget the fun times I was fortunate enough to spend rocking out and raising hell with you and the rest of Subject to Change. Rest n Punk, wild brother.

When John left college knowing he couldn't manage the stress his dad referred to him as a drop out and a loser for it. He had successfully completed a phlebotomy course but didn't work in the field. One because in our area finding this as a stand alone full time job isn't likely anymore and two he didn't end up wanting to do it long term. John only spent $750 on the course and still worked while he went to class. I know this weighed heavily on his mind. I've never wanted my kids to just sit around and be bums but I have encouraged them to find something you truly will enjoy doing for the long term. That may take some trial and error.

He worked hard and he either got past this or pushed it to the back of his mind.

He didn't have too many ups and down's during this school year except for the one night he didn't come home in time for school. There wasn't much I could except go to class myself and wait for him to contact me. I had gotten a smart phone by this time and he texted me around 9:00 to let me know that he had stayed with friends and awakened about ten minutes too late to move his car and it was towed. State College shows no mercy when it comes to parking. I spoke to my instructor, left to pick him up, took him to get his car and headed back to school and he got there shortly after.

In late March he came to me and asked to talk to me about something and told me at that point he'd been really thinking about a passion he'd had but not ever said much about. He said he was thinking he'd really like to work with kids and adults with learning disabilities. He'd actually started thinking about it when he was about twelve when we were at a museum in Philadelphia and a young man with a learning disability wanted to ride in a space flight simulator but couldn't go alone and his grandmother asked if John would like to go, her treat. He did and at that point he knew he felt moved for people like this but never said anything because he didn't want to be made fun of. He and I had briefly discussed it when he was in college when looking at add-ons for certifications but only briefly.

Anyway, his strongest point was that he never wanted people to be made to feel stupid for being different. I told him that I would support him in his decision but that he had to finish the precision machine program because he had to finish what he started and he had to finish it strong. I also suggested finding places to volunteer when school was finished so he could find out if this was going to be a good fit for him. He agreed on both counts and was pretty excited.

Around April he had a rock bottom day. He didn't want to go to the hospital. He though just a break from school stress for a day would be good, but he knew he shouldn't be alone. I couldn't miss more school so he rode in with me and just laid in the van and I checked on him every half hour or so. This started to seem stupid to me and I felt it wouldn't relieve any stress this way so I left class for the day. Things picked up and he seemed to be back on track.

He had spent a great deal of time with his close friend Jordan during this year and with friends from the band. He was very social all year. The school year appeared to everyone to be a good one for John. As always, he made friends easily at CPI and got along with his instructor and students from many different programs got to know him.

He completed the precision machine program and graduated on June 10, 2015.

His only disappointment was that he couldn't get his bow tie to tie correctly so he had to go with his traditional tie in a double Windsor knot.

Chapter 8

The Music of His Life

John found music and movement to be mesmerizing from a young age. He loved hearing music and on a trip to the Adirondack's when he was a toddler we saw a bluegrass band in a small setting. He was enthralled and walked right up to the front to dance by the band and was just amazed by the instruments. They loved him. That Christmas while at his grandma's in Buffalo while everyone else opened gifts he insisted on sitting at the organ pretending to play, pressing the keys, hoping for sound to come out. We had to open gifts for him because he had no interest other than that organ. He was finally allowed to turn it on. It's all he wanted to do the whole visit.

From the time he was about four he talked about wanting to play the piano. He'd play at my dad's house or wherever he'd see one. My mom had a small electric keyboard around her house and gave it to him to start on since buying a piano was out of the question. That was when he was about five. He would sneak down to the living room after bedtime and play it as quietly as he could with the hope of not being heard by us in the rec room below. Music was his obsession. I found a piano teacher. It was an acceptable "family expense" seeing it was five dollars a week. This started a love that would last a lifetime and end up being what took him to college. There are people who play the piano beautifully but John could feel the music and you felt his emotion pour out as he played. I so miss that sound in my home. That is one of the only things I regret, I don't have him recorded playing the piano and it breaks my heart.

He advanced quickly beyond the length of the small keyboard so I began looking for a second hand piano as reasonably priced a possible. I had a friend who wanted to find a new home for their family piano as her children were all grown. So she offered it to me for maybe two hundred dollars but that was still out of my reach. I grew up in a very music-centered home. My father and mother both can play the piano as does my brother. We ended up moving the piano into his room for a time because he played so often. I took lessons for a bit but gave it up. My father has an outstanding singing voice and performed in church and for years in local productions. My brother, dad and I all play trumpet as well, so music has always been important. When my dad found out about the opportunity he offered to buy the piano.

Once John had the full size piano keyboard his skill skyrocketed. He played for hours and it also became a stress reliever for him as well. When I would see him becoming upset about something or on edge I would suggest going to the piano.

He would and then play and play until he was relaxed. He soon would go on his own knowing his need for it. He never had to be prodded to practice his lessons. After seeing his grandfather perform with the Pittsburgh Symphony Orchestra on the trumpet, he had been chosen as part of a once a year event where private citizens could audition and a handful were chosen to perform for a night with the orchestra, John was in awe and said, "wow, that just makes me want to go home and practice something".

Seeing his aptitude for music, it was encouraged and nurtured. He, although homeschooled, went into the public school for saxophone lessons on a weekly basis around sixth grade. He was allowed to borrow an instrument. He liked it but it only lasted about a year. John used birthday money one summer to buy his first electric bass. He took to it right away. He had originally set out to get a guitar but at the store it was suggested that everyone gets a guitar why not think about a bass. Every band needs a bassist. So that's what he got.

He was self taught and usually learned songs he liked using tabs. We had stacks and stacks of printed out tabs piled up but he was actually really good. He started with a tiny, really tiny amplifier but quickly outgrew that, moved rapidly through sizes and ended up with a pretty big one that I helped him load and unload every Wednesday night for youth band. He started playing for the youth band at our church and quite liked performing and sharing the musical experience with other musicians. There was a young lady, Katelyn, with whom he played and of course he found her cute, but they just loved to play music. He helped introduce her to some musical things and being able to share the passion of music was incredible to him. We only lived about a mile away from their family and sometimes when it was a bad day he'd just go walking and show up at her house. He had to be reminded that he couldn't just do that. They played together for years.

Grampa always asked what musical thing he could get him for Christmas. First it was a mandolin. John had always loved the idea of a banjo but they were very pricey so he said a mandolin would be great too. He picked that up in nothing flat. The year he took two classes at the local high school (senior year) the assistant principal at the time found out he played the mandolin and when they got to talking asked John if he'd be interested in performing with him during the spring variety show the school put on. He jumped at the chance. They did a duet of Blue Moon of Kentucky with Mr. Briggs on guitar and John on mandolin and doing vocals. They started out at a slow tempo and then suddenly sped up and the crowd went wild. It was so much fun to watch. I sometimes watch it on my computer just for the smile and knowing it was the first time he had sung in front of an audience. I found out later that to make sure they were ready, the two of them had walked around the front office for a week before hand practicing in front of the administration. During the same variety show John and three friends recreated Metallica and played For Whom the Bell Tolls. They dressed up and had wigs and the song went over great especially because so many of the parents in the audience were teens when the song first came out. He had a blast that night. He said the next day at school he had lots of kids come up and say they had no idea he could play bass, or mandolin or sing. It was a very positive boost for him.

He acquired an electric guitar and an acoustic in short order, both of which he easily mastered. There was one point when the living room was really more of a music room filled with instruments and amplifiers. His sister began piano and percussion and added trumpet later and added violin. His brother took piano for two years but didn't want to continue. He ended up playing guitar, which he still plays. He has dabbled with John's bass but it is understandably too emotionally difficult most of the time. His bass became his emotional outlet and also helped release tension and frustration. During tense times he went right to it to play. I am sure it helped him through things no one will ever know.

He played different instruments at different times for different reasons. His sister's best friend Kathryn was around our house pretty frequently and John liked to hassle her in good fun like all big brothers do to little sister's friends. He liked to call her "troublemaker". She was always a good sport. Her brother, Thomas, was one of John's good friends also. John wandered around carrying his acoustic guitar sometimes just playing tunes and often when Evy and Kathryn were sitting on the porch swing John would go out and sit on the banister and join in the conversation. He'd take bits of what they were saying and make little stories and end the sentences with a chord. Something like, "Kathryn and Evy swinging and talking about ice cream, (chord)" and make them laugh. There is photo of him on the front porch with a cigarette dangling and a look of contentment on his face as he strums the acoustic. There is one of him performing on his bass in his blue striped button down with a wild look and there is one of him sitting on a log with Kayla, him in sunglasses wearing a brilliant smile looking at her as if there is nothing in the world but her as she plays a ukulele. There are four dates written on the side of his acoustic guitar. I have only discovered the significance of two and the others we may never discover but he gave those dates to his guitar and no one else.

As much as many of us were connected to John he was connected to nothing like he was to his music. To watch him perform was to truly understand him, if only for an instant. To watch his face when he played was to see a peace and contentment you didn't see at other times, even if you saw him sleep. His playing, especially piano, moved you. To John music was beauty, release, pain, hope, anger, joy, escape, imagination, wonder, possibility, tragedy, height, depth, healing, victory and perfection. He could express all of those things through his music without the need for lyrics or explanation. Music was being, for John.

Because of his connection to music and the way he was able to express himself and emote through his playing, like many artists with bipolar he feared that by controlling his illness with medications he would lose his musical abilities. (Touched With Fire, Jamison) We discussed this and I tried very hard to explain that this was very unlikely, but I don't ever think this fear left his thoughts.

Brad Parker
August 9:10 am

Yesterday I got some of the worst news I could imagine. This is a nightmare and we all need to wake up, but John, you were not only one of best friends and band mates, but you were a brother. I'll always remember the amazing times we've had over the past 5 years fondly, from yelling at TV screens of who the baby daddy was to jamming and turning our band into what it is today. Rest easy my brother and someday may we meet again. Love you bro.

The Band

Brad relays the history of the band. In 2010 he and John officially "met" at a Rock Studio concert, this was high school senior year for both of them. Brad was a student at Bellefonte High where John went for two classes. After the show John approached Brad to compliment him on his performance on the drums and after talking a while about what instruments John played they decided to jam together that fall. In the beginning their friend Alex was playing guitar, obviously John was the bassist but he also did vocals. Near the end of that December another friend Nick, also on guitar, joined. They played a lot of Blink 182 cover songs in the beginning. In the spring of 2011 they played miscellaneous stuff and then became much more serious that summer. His hospitalization in fall of 2011 was hard for everyone but they worked through it and Ethan, John's brother joined the band on guitar. Alex was no longer playing. There was a difficult situation in the band during the summer of 2012 and Nick was out of the band for a while due to some ruffled feathers. Romances can cause very tough times and mixed feelings.

Things got back on track with the band members and by the fall of 2013 they were a very serious band. They were doing a great deal of original songs, both lyrics and music, a large number of them coming from John. The band, Subject to Change, was doing some recording and by the summer of 2014, had cut their first album, Green Couch Sessions and were doing some shows. Things were consistently moving upward. In the summer of 2015 They had gigs that were taking them to places around Pennsylvania and they loaded my old green van with the equipment and took off for a couple of days at a time. Brad was working hard to get them work. At one of the last shows (it was a two part show) during the first set John was very stressed and Brad thinks he had been drinking and was not himself, messed up, was stressed. It wasn't very good. During the break though he seemed to have gotten it together and the second set was great. He was the performer everyone knew. I believe this was his last performance with the band.

Brad told me that he and John talked about his bipolar illness and John expressed great concern and fear about losing his musical ability if he were to get the illness completely under control with medications. As he had discussed with me, he was afraid that medications to even his moods would wipe out his creativity. It was greatly distressing for him.

He and I talked that summer about the band and how quickly they were going and their direction. He was concerned about the stress and the fast pace and what they could end up becoming. He never would have wanted to let the band down by leaving and didn't intend on doing so at that point but he said he had to really think about a lot of things down the road.

I loved hearing them practice in the basement. You hear people complain about "their blasted kids and their punk rock bands in the garage", but it was alive and wonderful. I liked having life in the house, activity and creativity going on right under my feet. They were happy, working together for a positive thing. Music is incredible and they were making it themselves, fresh and new, not replicating someone else's work, but pouring out something never before heard right from their hearts and minds.

The band continued on for a little over a year after the loss of John. A new young man, Jesse, became the bassist. Ethan took over vocals. It was hard to hear the first time. I sat on the front porch and cried just hoping to hear John's voice from the basement but it never came. It was nice to know it was his brother singing the songs and writing new ones. He wrote a beautiful tribute to John called Rosemary. The band put it on their second album.

The band is officially on hiatus, not broken up. Brad took a once in a lifetime job in Oregon, the other members have begun doing other things for awhile but getting together to play again, at least for fun, will happen at least for Evelyn's wedding. According to her.

Russ, from a band Greylines, approached John about performing a song that he had written. He thought it fit him and John liked the idea. I loved to hear him sing that song because it was as though the lyrics were coming straight from his heart. It did fit him wonderfully and he sang it with pure emotion. There are several recordings of it but I really like the one recording of it on the band's old Social Media page. I think it is probably because there is accompanying video and you can experience his presence.

Nick Fenix Pelick

I'm truly at a loss for words. My band mate, friend and most importantly brother passed away yesterday. I had known John Van Horn since high school and it's been history ever since. We've had our share of ups and downs but we always made it through. I was devastated when I sound out and was angry I couldn't be there for you in the end. But I know you're reppin StC with the angels now bro. Rest easy John, and hopefully someday we can meet again.

Jake Blass > John Van Horn

Johnny...man. I couldn't believe it when I heard it. I remember living with the band on 4th street and playing acoustic on the porch the night I met you. You came up and jammed and we clicked INSTANTLY. You are a hell of a guy and were always a kind and gentle soul. Rest easy brother. I know I'll see you again at that Great Gig In The Sky...

Red Slug

I see the struggle everyday.
I don't want to think or want to say.
When all you want is to break free.
Fuck you and your authority.

As days go by I watch the world die.
Plagued by this superficial life.
The tides that turn and wash against me.
Are filled with growing apathy.

All of the things we tried to be.
As far as all the eyes can see.
When I think of life I hold my breath.
What happens when there's nothing left?

As days go by I watch the world die.
Plagued by this superficial life.
The tides that turn and wash against me.
Are filled with growing apathy.

When will this madness go away.
We dream and hope for better days.
Against all odds we must contend.
We'll stand our ground until the end.

When will this madness go away.
We dream and hope for better days.
Against all odds we must contend.
We'll stand our ground until the end.

Russ Dauberman

A beautiful song written as a tribute to his brother:

Rosemary

Punk Rock was in the air, driving down the street without a care
Hopes and dreams in view, smoking cigarettes in your rusted blue
1981, chase the sky, the days go by
You were someone special, you were someone special

You were a loving friend
Touching hearts 'til the very end
You were a gift we won't forget

You'll never know what you meant to me
I know now you've been set free
Your laugh and smile will carry on

Raise your voice and sing, music is what gave you wings
Keep your song alive, the notes we play will help you fly
Step out into the night, look at the stars and see your light
Burning, still burning, we'll make sure it stays

Maybe I'll see you tomorrow
Maybe I'll see you tomorrow
Swore I'd see you tomorrow
Thought I'd see you tomorrow

You were a loving friend
Touching hearts 'til the very end
You were a gift we won't forget

You'll never know what you meant to me
I know now you've been set free
Your laugh and smile will carry on
Even though you're gone

Music by: Subject to Change
Lyrics by: Ethan Van Horn

Chapter 9

Turning Point

As discussed earlier and trying to be as brief as possible as this book is about John and not me and my relationship with his dad, it did however have an impact on things. I do not wish to upset my other two children as they have a right to form their own opinion about their father and some things I have kept private so as to prevent them from experiencing undue pressure to side with a parent or feel uncomfortable and I especially don't not want to cause hard feelings through the telling of John's story.

Prior to this our marriage had been strained and we held it together. I kept trying to work harder to be better. I had at times talked of splitting but my ex was very persuasive and quite convincingly explained that because of my "mental issues" I would never get the kids and he would make sure of that and on at least one other occasion I was clearly told that it would be easy to have me committed and put away where my parents would have to idea where to find me. I wanted nothing more than to be with my kids and care for them so I stayed. We ended up busying our selves with two of the kid's sports ambitions, which helped distract to a point. As they grew older it got harder to think of staying for the rest of my life and thoughts began to creep in that I could only do that if it could become a very short life. This became a warning sign to begin thinking of a way out. I had begun cutting to release the deep pain I was feeling, like screams I couldn't vocalize. I had hundreds of razor blade cuts on my lower calves and inner arms, which, I hid well. It is my hope that people will understand how words and behaviors crush spirits and alters a person's perception of themselves and reality.

Sometimes life becomes as simple as daily mental survival. I reveal this information only because I may have continued to stay until the event that changed my perspective happened one summer afternoon in 2013. John had been hospitalized for a short time that spring but was doing pretty well. He was working at the Dollar General Store in town where he was well liked by his employer, coworkers and customers.

John's dad and I were in the kitchen with John having a discussion. It wasn't an argument. I don't think it was even very negative really just maybe about John not getting enough hours at work, but nothing earth shattering or maybe that he needed to find a direction since he had left college at that point. Anyway John went out the kitchen door, headed across the side yard to his car at the top of the yard. Through the window we watched him go and although I cannot remember the entire exchange

of words I distinctly remember his dad say, "I'm done, I can't love him anymore."
I replied asking what he meant, saying that it's unconditional love with your child, and he said something like, "no, not him, I can't love him", he had had enough and couldn't love him. It was at that moment I truly believe my heart hardened toward him. There was no repairing it. John had never tried to harm his father, spoken ill of him, had even a seriously heated argument with him, stolen from him or any of a number of things one might expect a father to be furious about but would still love a son through. I think he saw his son as damaged goods. It was then that triggered the beginning of the end of our marriage.

Chapter 10

From Bad to Good and Back

John had come a long way since his dad had left the house. Each person dealt with his departure differently, but I will focus mainly on John and how he grew. His dad and I had been legally separated since October of 2013 but he didn't physically move out of the house until May of 2014 so it was a very volatile situation most of the time or one of cold silence. This didn't help John. I had wanted his dad to go immediately when he finally knew I would not change my mind about the divorce but he didn't work that way so it had to go according to his plan.

It was not an easy leaving or starting over but those details are not necessary. That summer was difficult for the relationship between John and his brother. There was a tension there, which had never been there before. John had quickly decided to cut all ties with his father as soon as he was out of the house. He didn't want to see him or really even talk about him. He talked to me about it a lot. We spent hours on the porch swing talking about the past, feelings, his hopes, healing and fears, things he didn't share with his siblings about his dad. I have learned he did speak frequently with Erin about this subject and with Kayla a long-time girlfriend. He discussed with me that he had decided to refer to his dad by his first name rather than dad because he said, "it helps me forget whom he is to me and helps me heal". I don't think even I knew what was in his head about his dad. He would be gracious and go with his brother and sister to his dad's for a bonfire occasionally that first summer because they wanted him to. I know that Ethan would often ask John to go with him to a restaurant with him and his dad or to the house and John would always decline. Finally it came to a head and John quite forcefully told his brother something like 'he didn't want to go spend time with the man and didn't he remember what he did to our family and for Ethan to never ask him again'. It was hard for Ethan because he was the peace keeper and wanted to keep a connection with his dad and be close to his brother and I don't think he understood where John was coming from. Each child sees their parent's relationship and the relationship their parent has with their siblings from a totally different perspective and this was a slap in the face to Ethan. Evy fell somewhere in between on the spectrum and kept out of this completely, besides it was between brothers and hers is her own story.

John had been on and off of medications and tried to self medicate with alcohol and marijuana and as we later learned some opioids. Good things were going on with the band as described elsewhere and he always had his music but behind the scenes always his mind was always sabotaging him. Contrary to what people believe the holiday season does not see the highest suicide/attempt rate. It is actually the summer. July of 2014 was John's worst episode we had ever dealt with.

I had come home from working a temporary summer job in the behavioral health field and found John down in his room on his bed very lethargic appearing to have been drinking and possibly have taken something. He had done this before and usually I would talk to him and ask if he wanted to go the hospital and he'd calmly say, "Yeah, mama, I need to go to the hospital". This time was different. He didn't want to tell me what he took, or communicate for a while. I could tell it wasn't immediately life threatening or I would have called an ambulance. I sat with him and finally was able to get him to tell me he'd been drinking and had taken Klonipin, although a dangerous mix he hadn't taken many and had done it several times before. I kept trying to convince him to go to the hospital and gave him a bit of time to think while I went up to change and then his brother got home and I talked to him. By the time I came back down John had apparently completely finished off a pint of homemade apple liquor a coworker had made and given him and grabbed the car keys. Ethan was in the yard trying to keep him from getting in the car and they almost came to blows, something that had never happened before and never happened again. They came back inside and all keys to all cars were promptly hidden and we tried to calm him. He had never before been agitated like this. I called the "Can Help" line, a hotline for emergency emotional help because I didn't want to call the police knowing that would only make him more scared and agitated. They said they'd send an assessment person out but that I should call the police. I cried while doing it.

We are in a small town so I called the non-emergency number instead of 911 and explained the situation and begged them not to put lights and sirens on to avoid upsetting him because he wasn't violent. They kindly did as I asked and even parked on the side lot instead of the driveway. He was sitting on the porch and quickly got upset that they were coming and asked if I called them. I blamed it on the Can Help people honestly in hopes of keeping him less mad at us. All the police did was walk up on the porch and start chatting with him and tell him they just wanted to make sure he was feeling okay and see if there was anything they could do. He was quite calm by then. He used to buy pipe tobacco and cigarette papers and roll his own cigarettes because it was cheaper so he began rolling a cigarette with the last tiny bit of flakes he had left and the officer looked a bit wide eyed and inquired as to what he was doing. After he explained the officer laughed and said he was a little taken aback at first. When the Can Help lady arrived the police officers left when they cleared with her that it was okay.

After doing an assessment she told him he needed to go to the hospital because he was a threat to himself. Strangely though, he didn't want to go. He also admitted to drinking about a third of a bottle of rubbing alcohol on top of the pills and alcohol he ingested before I got home and then the stuff from the fridge. The assessment woman explained that if he didn't go on his own she would have to do an "involuntary" admittance because of how high he was scoring on his assessment. She gave me time to talk with him. I tried to explain to him that he needed to check himself in for a lot of reasons but the one that was most convincing to him was that having an involuntary hospitalization on his record could make it hard for him in the future for many things, especially when it came to certain career choices and that was about the only thing that would convince him. Ethan and I took him up in my van and the woman said to put him in the back with the child locks in place, which really startled us. As we neared the hospital he started jerking on the handle of the door and then pushing through toward the front seats. At the entrance I got out and walked him to the ER doors while Ethan parked, I didn't need him to have an altercation with his brother. It was a few days before Ethan wanted to visit at the hospital.

John knew how much he had hurt Ethan through all of that and asked to have

their mutual friend, Jordan be sort of a mediator when he got home so he and his brother could talk it all out and come to some kind of truce. They did and I don't think there was ever an issue again. He also wrote a heartfelt letter to Jordan apologizing for almost leaving the world and what a mistake that would be. He let me read it after John's passing. He keeps it in his vehicle and believes strongly that it's John's way of telling him he didn't choose to go.

After this hospitalization John worked on staying on medications. He stayed sober for a pretty long time. He asked me to go through his stuff and make sure he didn't have anything stashed and to have everything cleared out before he was discharged. While he was in the hospital this time the guys from the band came over and we all talked in the driveway for a long time. They were always supportive and cared a great deal about John. They visited him and said they had been worried about him. They agreed he needed to do whatever he had to because they didn't want to out on the road doing a show and come back to the room and find him gone. I know they put up with big mood swings from him and probably bad attitudes but also super crazy musical highs as well.

He got on track after that huge crash. The fall of 2014 all four of us enrolled in school together and it was quite a year. We all attended different programs at the same technical school, The Central Pennsylvania School of Science and Technology. His time there was explained during his educational experience.

So although there had been a hospitalization in the summer of 2014 right after he was discharged John kind of kicked it up a notch. He began to step into a new role. He felt a freedom to do things he hadn't before, not like a kid who goes to college and goes out partying but things most people don't think about. He began offering to do jobs around the house, tasks he would never have tried before, working on his car and just diving into the unknown because he didn't fear the consequences, according to him. He wasn't worried about being too stupid to do it right or of messing it up. He had a new confidence. He began being self-assured and his attitude was "if it doesn't work this time we'll try something else". He was a breath of fresh air on some days when I thought I would sink. We got sewage backup in the basement and he pretty much jumped right in to tackle it but suggested we, "take off our shoes mama so they don't get ruined". He seemed unsinkable. He was always lifting up everyone and could get anyone to laugh even in the worst possible situation. It was another one of his gifts. A favorite saying of his, if everything else had failed to cheer you up in a bad situation was, "well, at least you don't have lava on your face" and it never failed to do the trick. It was so much fun to watch. Others saw it too. He had fun. Friends came over and he and Ethan and Jordan played Playstation hockey in the basement for hours. They could be loud in the house all they wanted and it was okay. I loved it. I loved hearing fun! We had bonfires in the side yard every week and John played his acoustic guitar and everyone sang. Their friends knew they were welcome, anytime. One evening two friends, Jordan and Sean stopped, looking for John but he wasn't home. I was working on the bathroom renovation and they stayed and helped tear out plaster with me for an hour.

It was comfortable. There was peace among the busyness. His was the voice I loved to hear when I was in doubt. The lilt in his words, "It's okay Mama, we'll figure it out", always lightened the situation. I long to hear the sound of his feet coming up the stairs toward my room to say those words of reassurance. I fear I'll forget the sound of his voice. I just want to sit on the side of my bed hoping he'll peek around the corner, but he never does.

The school year had this kind of feel throughout, one of new freedom mixed with new responsibility. It was a very unique experience. John and I learned a lot about each other that year, especially that spring going into summer. Near the end of spring his moods were varied and he seemed to be cycling rapidly. I think he had all but given up on medications. He had been using marijuana to help with his extreme anxiety and stress for a while and was successfully controlling some of the really bad attacks. I am not giving a blanket recommendation for medical marijuana use but I would like to see research opportunities for bipolar patients. He had unfortunately begun drinking some again but I don't believe it was as heavily as it had once been or the hard liquor it had been. I could see that his mind was very tortured near the beginning of the summer and he seemed as though he might be headed toward a manic episode.

This was confirmed when he came home from a night out with friends and told me he had dropped six hundred dollars treating his friends to a fun night. He said he couldn't help it and that he knew he should stop but just couldn't. He asked me to take him to the bank and have them make sure he couldn't access his account on his own and even explained to them that he had an illness. They were very nice and made a note on the account. He was able to get things under control again.

John he wrote this one day as a reminder
to himself and hung it above his bed.

Chapter 11

His Last Summer

We had all graduated together in June and everything was settling down pretty much on the home front and we had gotten it figured out for the most part as a family of four. It had been a tough but good year all in one. I unexpectedly became suddenly ill and landed in the hospital with a tonsil abscess. It took three visits to the ER before they would keep me and John was getting pretty mad about the lack of attention I was receiving. I hadn't eaten for a week and spit in a cup rather than swallowing because the pain was excruciating. They kept giving me IV's for hydration and sending me home. I have a weird resistance to pain meds so I was miserable. I finally ended up staying for five days on IV dilaudid and IV antibiotics. Was discharged July 3.

July 4th had arrived. He loved holidays. This happened to be his last and he grabbed his skateboard, Kurt sunglasses and dirty Vans and hopped in the car with Evelyn and her boyfriend at the time, Bryan to head up to "Fourth Fest". They snapped a photo and it is a favorite of Evy's because they are making the same face and they had a great time that whole day.

He was all over the place that summer, friends came and went, and we had bonfires. I have pictures of him, Ethan, Jordan and Evy playing football in the side yard and acting like little kids. If one had known it was his last summer you would have thought he was living it the best he knew how. I have a great picture of him in his beat Vans, sloppy cargo shorts, and sweaty tank with a dangling cigarette, wearing my required safety glasses holding the weed whacker and a beer next to the driveway. It makes me smile just remembering how helpful and goofy he was.

Part way through the summer he started to do side work for his friend Brian. It was hard work, physical work. He was helping do replacement windows, learning drywall, and construction basics, that kind of thing. He came home one evening and said how much he enjoyed it. He said it was hard and tiring but it made him feel like he was really working and getting a job done. He seemed very content on those days. It was a good physical stress reliever.

I think John was the kind of person who could find a bit of his purpose in everything he did. It was definitely a gift he had. Few people can find a way to be content in everyday life and even fewer can at such a young age. Deep down he was never really content as I learned from his writing but on good days I think he was or he was good at coming across that way.

Unfortunately his mind was fighting him at the same time. It was destroying his ability to think rationally and believe he could keep going. He was doing his best to overcome but the mind is extraordinarily powerful. He did a great deal of journaling that summer and it is incredible how quickly his mood shifted. When I came across the writings I was not sure if I could read them. I'm glad I did because amidst the pain I found incredible beauty that was the true heart of my son who wrestled so desperately against the demons, trying to get the upper hand. One of the summer pictures is of him standing on the porch. He's in a green pullover I sewed for him and he is looking toward the camera.

To most people it's a nice photo of John. I hate this picture. I see behind his eyes a sorrow, a look of pleading to be released from the pain and internal turmoil he is silently suffering. As you read his journal entries you can feel his jumps in mood and how he is struggling against himself.

He began the journal in spring, approximately early March of 2015 and the last entry in July of the same year and the drastic changes in that short time frame are frequent and quite extreme at times. The rush of the manias could even been seen in his erratic handwriting.

Written on the cover of his journal is *"Somewhere in the between was a life of which we all dream, and nothing and no one will ever take that away"*, lyrics from a Streetlight Manifesto song.

These are some of the entries from his final journal:

This entry must have been written at the Susquehanna River near LHU

Entry 1: *So I guess I'm back where it all began. Christ the river look different at the beginning of spring. Logs, the swifter current, hell the ice chunks that have gotta be at least twice the size of me, it's a completely surreal sight in comparison to those late September days. The cloud cover is strikingly similar, yet the cool autumn rain is so distinct that nothing could make you forget it. Three and a half years later still feels like yesterday. All those thoughts and feelings came rushing back; even the cold in my fingers feels the same.*

I still dread returning to this place. I can feel the tears in my eyes, on my face, as I write down what I thought were going to be my last pained words. Remembering knowing that the shock would wear off and I would become a distant memory of a troubled kid who couldn't handle the overpowering weight of his world. I never realized that on that dreary day would start a struggle that I am most likely going to have to endure the rest of my life. Oh how I wish that I could control it. Even Icarus, with the knowledge of what he possessed still let it overcome him. I just kept soaring higher and higher wanting to feel that rush, not caring that at any moment my wings will melt and I come crashing back into the sea like always.

I will never understand how to control it. No matter how much I want to, it will always be the jar atop the fridge. I've slowly learned the patterns though. If only it didn't take fucking this God damn long. All I can say is thank Jesus that I can see what's coming next.

Entry 2: *I have no idea what to write about this time. You ever just kinda think? I think too much all the time. That, or my mind completely shuts off, completely vacant. Why as a species are we meant to have complex thought?*

All I know is that when I'm not thinking I'm filled with apathy and am totally jaded. On the other hand, it's sometimes a nice change to the rush, rush, rush of thoughts and ideas, both good and bad. Christ, I have so much going on through my head it's so difficult to sort everything out and I just want to act on it all and do everything.

Right now, I want to quit school, become a vagrant across the country. I want to hear everyone's story, their lives, who they are. I want to take my shitty ass guitar and write awful sounding songs about them. Just to take every day as it is, more playing, sleep in parking lots and do things for people in exchange for a warm meal and a roof. God, that all probably sounds insane. I don't think I'll ever be content. I feel like no matter what I was born in the wrong place at the wrong time. Just music, people, exploring. I realized today that everything is temporary. Possessions have the ability to posses you. I was so enraged that two cuts went missing today.

It doesn't matter though, weed doesn't have thoughts, a car can't tell you that it's owner's father was emotionally abusive and would drive it to escape that. Yeah, objects have stories, but those stories are never going to be known unless they are told by another living, breathing person.

Every single person (unreadable) that has a story, or an experience, but only they can portray the exact feeling. That's why I think I get so depressed at estate auctions. Those things are the most memorable objects that that one person owned. I do love some of the things I own but those memories of events

last far longer than any thing we will own.

Entry 3: *Man I wish I didn't love being in love so much. I just kinda hits you how lonely you are sometimes. More often than not those thoughts creep out at me when I'm laying here. I feel like sometimes I shouldn't be so affectionate.*

I absolutely love the feeling of waking up beside the same person each day. I'm always in we each time they're asleep still, amazed that I get to wake up next to them and get to fall asleep together. Fuck, just contact like holding hands, and just seeing them laugh and smile, it's the most fulfilling feeling. There isn't much that measures up to that, really the only thing after that is music.

Sigh, I'm so tired of the heartbreak. As much as it hurts, it makes me happy that at least Kayla and Chloe are n such amazing places. It makes me so happy that I got to spend time with them and know them deeply. I let them truly know me and who I am. Knowing that I was a part of their journey to where they're at today fills me with nearly inexplicable feelings. I do feel slightly saddened from the thought of being alone, but just life is such a bizarre trip full of things that if we learn to just enjoy them will blow us away. Why be sad your whole life? Why not just see that every second you have you're on a planet where there are just the right gases and environment to support you.

Even the slightest changes during its formation, and everything is different. The chance of being here is the luckiest shit. Also billions of others are just like you, yet you are the only one that can feel every experience differently.

Damn, I really got off topic and I don't think that any of that is pertinent. Oh well, at leas I get to write.

Entry 4: (partial-I've excluded a portion that could be very hurtful to someone) *I hate my mind sometimes. The mix of my childhood, relationships and the disorders. I still sidestep the fact that I'm bipolar, I don't know how anyone will react. Hell, acceptance and tolerance for so much else is so much higher than for mental illness. I don't want people to shun me, I don't want them to act differently around me. Understanding is all I truly want. I want everyone to be ok with me saying I don't want to do anything except be in my bed. For them to understand my manic episodes, how racy and unpredictable and impulsive I get.*

Maybe one day they will. I think…I think that's why I'm always drawn to girls that have their own demons. I want them to fully know me, be there for me and I want to know them, and be there for them when they struggle with those demons. I've always taken the supportive role my entire life, my mom, my sister, my relationships.

... Now all I do with confrontation is withdraw instantly. I hate arguments, being in them, hearing them, even from complete strangers.

When you fall asleep to them almost every night for twenty-two years you never want another argument again. I don't know if I'll ever be able to withstand them. All I know is how to absorb it. I don't like feeling completely hopeless, but I don't want to hurt anyone. I'd much rather be the one who's hurt, I've been so used to it all these years. I know I can get back up from it, and I know that if I were to argue back I would take it too far.

I know everything is gonna work out. Maybe not today or tomorrow, but everything's gonna be all right in the long run.

Entry 7: *(he had to have been in a manic episode at the time)*

The mind is a terrible thing. Out of all the things I've done and seen, the mind had the ability to make you unknowingly feel things both physically and mentally. When my mind rushes like this, my body rushes.

Why does the body have this, this insane power? Fuck, it's fucking annoying. I feel so ungrounded right now. I want to be able to take advice better. I've always been able to give advice no problem, but vice versa it's impossible.

I think of Chloe, everything I told her, and did. I want so much to be able to listen and release myself from my mind. I'm the lightest I've been, everyone can see it and says I look great, but all I can see are fucking scars and stretch marks and everything that I don't want to see.

I see and feel the scars each time it's cold, feel them during every shower. I fear so much everyone can see them. In all honesty, I don't ever feel like I'll be happy with myself physically and mentally. This episode doesn't help. I can't eat or sleep, people keep asking if I'm on something.

It's getting harder to play it off. At the same time though, I missed this shit. Fuck, did I miss it. I missed the weightlessness, the soaring, I feel like a bird. I've always hoped that it there was the slightest chance of reincarnation that I would be a bird, and never let this feeling go away.

Entry 8: *...Even outside of relationships I still remember the things and stories that made someone happy.*

Brad and his stories of Oregon, how much my sister loves penguins, hell, even how my therapist talks about her husband. It all makes me happy. As much as I don't get people, I love knowing the unknowable them. Humans are a funny breed, you have no idea how much they intimidate me, yet excite me and put me into a state of pure marvel.

I just...I want everyone to know that sincerity is so easily falsified at times, and that the beauty each of us has is sometimes withdrawn. If we loved the human race, or who they are, there would be no need for ridicule and stigma. Just because someone is an outcast for how they look or act, doesn't mean that they aren't a beautiful soul.

We all have been raised in this fucked up here and now you need to fuckin' mess with me off the bat or fuck you, you God damn punk world. Maybe if you slowed the fuck down you'd realize we both lose our minds over dachshunds, or love the morning after a storm and sitting on the still damp grass not giving a damn that it's a little cold and our asses are soaked. Live life, enjoy your time here. That's the one great thing about life, none of us gets out alive, so, don't take it too seriously.

Entry 9: (He is most likely writing this entry as if talking to the late Kurt Cobain) *I guess it was only a matter of time before I wrote in here while I'm real fucked up and not in a good place. Christ I'm so tired. My body is feeling so Goddamn worn, and my head just can't stop and rest.*

Kurt I wish I knew what runnin through your head. Fuck, you just, you couldn't beat it. You couldn't see it all, and the drugs and your head wouldn't let you. I know what it's like man, not to ? How big everything got for you. My life is fucked up, my childhood, my relationship, right now man even.

I just want to meet you one day, and just be us to each other. To hear your stories, and for you to hear mine. I just worry man. I get to thinking what's gonna happen to me? There's a very high chance of me going out in a bad way.

But like, I love life, life's beautiful. It's my head, man, who I am fucks it. Then I start drinking, or pills and part of me wants to go back to killers, or worse. That feeling of it, it's indescribable. I'm here but I'm not. I'm in a real bad place man…real bad.

Entry 10: *It feels good to be out of Bellefonte. The air here is different, even the hills. It's so much the same, but it's all strange and unfamiliar. I wish I could run away. Sigh, as good as it feels to be away, all those thoughts and () are still in the back of my mind.*

I get to thinking about school and everyone I care about, and I just wanna change the world and I don't think I can. …….. This getaway is gonna help, maybe I'll be able to figure some stuff out. I'm gonna do it, I'm gonna see about that ARC (organization for people with disabilities) so that volunteer work.

I say that, but will it ever happen? I'm so damned. I honestly don't know how much more I've got in me. I wish I'd remembered sweatpants. (He was known for his randomness) I hope Chloe's making it through. Someone's gotta keep fighting.

Entry 11: (partial)

Today I'm feeling a little bit better. It's still a fuckin' battle and I still don't know the outcome of me...

Entry 12: *This weekend is almost through. I still don't know how I feel about it. I don't want to drive home, or have that realization that everything is still there. I've always kinda wanted to run away, just drop off for a while. Still feels like I'm losing it.*

Entry 13: *Today is the first day of my life. 4/14/15.*
(This is one of the dates written on his guitar.)

Entry 14: (Apparently he had met and spoken to someone the one night and they talked and he opened up to her and this was his entry in response to it...)
After that I realized that's who I wanna be for the rest of my life, this young punk who just loves the human race, and wants to change the whole world.

I don't know exactly where to start, but the music is gonna help, and I know now that in any way, shape or form, I'm gonna help anyone who's in need. I want everyone to see that this world, this life, is absolutely fuckin beautiful, and it doesn't matter who or what you are, you should do even the smallest things for everyone. I want this needless me, me, me mindset to end. To break down the walls each of us has decided to erect between one another.

I have such high aspirations for this world, for people. This only thing holding us back is us. I'm not being held back anymore.

Entry 16:

Let's go outside,
It's a beautiful day,
It's a beautiful life.

Entry 17: *...It's funny how fast things can change. Life is this really strange trip, and I think I'm starting to get it a little bit after all these years. I finally am starting to feel happy again. I'm thinking in the next few days of heading to State (State College) and just playing guitar for a while, maybe somebody'll stop and just kinda chill and I get to know them.*

Their hopes, dreams, fears. Even just for a moment, even if we never cross paths again, jus to be part of their life, to listen. Man I probably sound completely outta my mind to anyone that'd read this. People, being around them, not being superficial and seeing who they are truly. I sorta realize that after all these years of wanting stability, consistency, that stability always meant pain.

Deep down, I think that what I've always needed that chaos of not knowing what's next, but now knowing how to just roll with it, it's what I've always needed. I've always tried fighting it for years and now I'm finally getting it. Everyone's always said that I've always been the most random person they've ever known. Evy told me that she always knew that I was gonna be a vagabond, I think Mom would understand it. I heard Seattle is nice; I'm sure theirs some nice people on the way.

Entry 18: *Today was a good day. I got a couch outta riff raff. I finally have my boy back. This weekend overall was awesome possum. Greylines and Russ rocked. It was wicked rad.* (*Riff raff is a week each spring when the whole town puts stuff out for trash and it's taken by the trash people for free and it doesn't matter the size. So people troll around for great finds like John's couch, which by the way was very clean and comfortable. *His "boy" was most likely his good friend Jordan returning from college for the summer. *Greylines is a band that often played when their band did and Russ is a member.)

Entry 19: *Today I'm really struggling. Just…I really don't know what to do…I feel like this is the beginning of the end, but I'm gonna hold on as long as I can. I'm so fucking sorry…*

Entry 22: *There are times I wish I had someone to sit next to. This loneliness is so crippling at times, but I know I have a lot of shit going on, and shit I need to work on about myself. I mean, fuck it's be nice to get to hold someone, fall asleep holding them, but I couldn't do it just to say that I have someone.*

The pills help a bit. I'm still lonely, but I feel…ok. I feel that warm comfort, and damn did I miss it. I know I can't do it for long, and I know if I ever got to H…. I'd be in love, more than anyone I've ever loved. I really don't know if I'd ever do it. I could never let Mom or Evy or Kayla and Erin down.

As much as I know I missed my chance, .I'm still crazy about Erin. That first love always sticks with you. It fucking sucks cause I know it'd never happen. I should've kissed her when I could have. She was always there, she never gave up on me, and I've always believed in her. Maybe I should stop thinking about it, maybe there's someone out there that comes close to the person she is.

Entry 23: *Looks like I'm writing some more self pity bullshit tonight. Christ, I* *was really hoping that July was gonna be different this year. I told myself that it was gonna be. Thank fuck that I feel X this time around.*

I really need to write lyrics tomorrow; maybe I can use Erin as some inspiration. She will always be an inspiration to me. I don't think she'll ever realize how much of a hero she is to me. It's so wonderful to see her smile and to just see her and know her.

My addiction is getting worse, it's never been this bad. I'm on such a spiral, She's never given up hope, and I don't ever want her to feel like that was a huge mistake.

Entry 25: (Written 4 times in several angles on the page in all capitals)
DEATH DON'T SEEM SO BAD SOMETIMES

Entry 26: *I don't wanna do this. Why am I so piss ass poor at every fucking thing? What the fuck did I fucking do? Was just being fucking born the thing that set all this fucking shit into a constant spiral? Or, you know, the fact that at any given time that I even remotely have an inkling that there's a possibility that I might be happy, it doesn't fucking matter "cause I'm a horrible piece of shit that always fucks up every Goddamn thing?*

I see how many people have their shit together. My shit? The only fucking constant is agonizing and a fucking cruel joke that's me trying to get things right and failing. How many more years is it gonna be? Nothing is gonna change. At the end of every day it's just gonna be me, and every morning is gonna be the same thing: waking up grasping a fucking pillow.

I can't even off myself. It can't be that fucking hard, but nope, still manage to fuck that up too. Why did I promise Erin that I'd stay alive? I can't break a promise to her. I'm just such a fucking idiot all the time. It's all gonna get snatched away, and all that's gonna be left is cold and dark. I can't fucking write correctly. All I'm good for is for everyone to fucking worry about me…

This was John's final entry in his last journal.

Chapter 12

From the Outside Looking In

Pretty much everybody saw John differently than he saw himself. I love the stories others share about John and how he touched their lives, whether it was for years or for just a few moments. This is what made John the incredible, positive person he was and it's one of the main reasons I felt compelled to write this book. Because of him lives were changed, for the better. I am not just saying that, people have told me that after his death they paused and rethought how they were living their lives and because of the way he so deliberately lived his they changed parts of theirs. This is incredible to me.

I know I've tried to make changes. I began to keep a daily journal and before I make any other entry for the day I write three things for which I am thankful and one thing in which I found beauty that day. They can be things as simple as being thankful for fuzzy blankies or that I saw beauty in the way the mortar looked curling around the bricks on the house while I was sitting on the porch. This is how he tried to live everyday, even in the bad times. Few people saw the bad times because he was so intent on making sure everyone else was having good times.

To share what others saw is vital in sharing John. My friend Brenda lives in a location where her back deck is visible from the road and she told me that one afternoon, out of the blue John pulled into the driveway and walked around the back of the house and on to the deck where she was sitting and told her he had seen her from the road and it looked like she could use a hug so he thought he'd better stop and give her one. She said it meant the world to her because she is no longer able to drive due to a brain injury and doesn't get out much and having him think of her when her saw her sitting there just in passing was enormous. She said he stayed a few minutes and then he had to get to work or someplace and headed out.

Erin tells many great stories because of the amount of time they spent together. They were on one of their frequent Sheetz (a gas station/convenience chain) late night snack hang-out sessions and although John thought himself shy he was anything but. Erin said that as they sat at one of the outside tables John would talk to everyone coming or going and ask how they were or comment on something. He struck up a conversation with a guy one night about a band tee shirt he was wearing that ended up lasting almost an hour she said once they started talking about albums and songs and band members.

My favorite Sheetz story has to be the one about the time John first met Erin's friend Sam. He was chatting with them and commented that his jeans had a huge rip in them. All of a sudden John said," I can fix that", jumped up, got that wide-eyed, goofy, open-mouth smile that meant "I have an idea", bounded over to his car and rushed back with something in his hand. Reached out and slapped a big piece of duct tape on Sam's pants. The thing is it wasn't any old duct tape it was light blue with pickles on it and it said, "dill with it". So Sam thanked him and John said, "It's not a big dill". That was the only time Sam met John and when Erin told him of John's passing he said, wait, the pickle guy?" and was really surprised and sad.

I think some of my all time favorite stories from Erin is of John and her son Bryson. John adored Bryson and I remember him coming home and telling me how excited he was that Erin was going to have him some years before. He asked if we could make him a baby blanket, out of polar fleece with the name embroidered in the corner, like I often did for people. I said yes, for sure. He picked the fleece, it had cute sharks on it, and he sewed the edges himself so he could say he made it and I did the name. As Bryson grew John was determined that someday he would teach him to play guitar. Erin has a fabulous phone video of John playing his acoustic guitar at her house and Bryson, who was about four at the time walked over and reached out to strum the strings and John says, "Go ahead", then Bryson strums and John changes chords so it sounds like a song and Bryson's eyes get huge and he stops for a second and John tells him to, "keep going buddy, you're doing great", and then Bryson tells his mom, "look mom, I'm, really playing!" and she says something like, "you sure are"! Bryson gave John a sticker to put on that guitar and he did. He never took it off and said he never would. He was so proud of that sticker and posted a picture of it n Social Media. It will stay there.

It is nice to know that Bryson remembers John. Erin says he points to the family photo wall that contains a photo of her and John and he says, "That's John" and she'll ask if he remembers him and he does. I do think my favorite story is of, as she tells it, the day Bryson called him "Uncle John" for the first time. He had gone up to visit and Bryson said he wanted to play Hungry, Hungry Hippos so John was setting up the game at a little table and meanwhile Bryson had climbed up on John's back and fallen asleep. Erin came in and saw John leaning over the game with Bryson sound asleep on his back and asked why he didn't put him down somewhere and John said he seemed too comfortable to move him. He stayed that way for a long time just so the little guy could nap. She snapped a photo and it's included among the pictures in the back. It's just the kind of person he was.

A middle-aged woman came to the funeral home and introduced herself to me. She said that she had known John only from the time period he had worked at the Dollar General store in town. She went on to say that at first she was always warmed by his great smile and friendliness but then he would always ask how she was and she realized that he truly was interested in knowing. During the time he worked there she would go in and they would talk and she said she knew he listened and was genuinely caring and took the time with her. She said occasionally she would just think of something to go to the store for that she didn't really need just to talk with him. She expressed that she just wanted me to know how much that he meant to her and that I should know.

There have been so many stories like this that warm my heart. I don't think anyone who met him ever forgot him. It's just incredible.

Chapter 13

The Chapter I Don't Want to Write

July 10, Text

John: *I love you Mumma*

Me: *I love you too poo*

It was nearing the end of July and John rescued an injured bat one morning but had to go to work. I was supposed to head to Pittsburgh that afternoon for my 30th high school class reunion but I quickly drove it to Centre Wildlife Care so it could be saved and home again to get set to leave.

July 25, Text

Me: *I should have just enough time to get there and back and get ready and to Pittsburgh in time.*

John: *Okey dokey mumma*

He was in good spirits with us and we were having fun those days. He was his silly self and always was sure to give me a hug and kiss. Apparently he had recently heard a story about a pig that had escaped butchering and ran away because he had known what was coming so John decided he was going to become a vegetarian. So I was going to the grocery and had asked him if he wanted me to get special things for him so he had texted "Nah, just get the regular stuff". Erin tells me she had heard the story from him too and told him he was no vegetarian and he had decided he just wouldn't eat pork since he felt bad for that pig. I texted him to let him know I'd be home within a half hour and asked if he wanted watermelon (THE watermelon that comes into play later) and he texted back "sure thing".

August 2, 2015 at 7:22 pm

John: *I'm heading to Snow Shoe so use Social Media if ya need me. (no service)*

Me: *Otay. Jordan ended up driving E. (Ethan) No Biggie. Red van's better anyway. Not like I had a date. Ha. Be careful, have fun.*

(John's car needed to be inspected so he had taken my red van so I didn't have a car for the night. Ethan and Jordan went somewhere in Jordan's car)

This was my last ever communication with my son.
Erin described the evening they had together playing like kids at first.

"The last night we had together was a really fun time. He had come up (Snowshoe) after work. We were all cleaning out our cars and just listening to music. When he got there we started playing cards in the driveway and drinking and talking and telling stories and laughing so hard my sides were hurting. During the game of Kings Cup is when he really started to change. I noticed he was getting snippy, and wasn't acting like himself. So I tried to take the alcohol away from him. He got really mad at me, and crawled under Brian's van. He actually fell asleep under there and we all figured it would be better to let him sleep. A couple hours later, everyone was getting ready to leave and we decided we had to wake him up. When we woke him up he tried to get his key to drive home. I told him I wouldn't allow it, and that we were going to drive him. He tried to fight everyone for his keys, but we were able to take them from him. He then stripped his flannel off and threw it at us and ran off. We found him laying on the hill just up from my house. We all talked to him to get him to calm down, and I remember telling him how much I loved him and needed him to be home safe and that's why we needed to take him and not let him drive. We put him in Brian's van, so that I could drive the other one (yours) down."

Brian drove with John and Erin followed behind in my van. Later Brian explained to me that John was agitated the whole drive home, and seemed angry. This was not like John. He kept messing with the door handles and window controls and Brian kept telling him he was getting him home to his mom and it was going to be okay, just hang on. He was doing his best to drive and keep John under control. Brian said he seemed panicked and after a time was able to get the window down even with him (Brian) pushing the "up" button as often as possible. He said John suddenly looked over at Brian and said, "I have to go right now", and went out the window.

Ethan woke me up at about 1:30 a.m. and said that I needed to come downstairs because there was a policeman at the door. I didn't think much of it. I got to the kitchen and stepped on to the porch and he said I needed to go to Altoona hospital right away because there had been an accident involving my son John. When I asked what happened he said all he was told was to tell me to go to the hospital. I think he probably knew everything but wasn't supposed to upset me.

I still don't think I was really too upset yet, I don't know why. I asked if Ethan wanted to go and he did and I woke Evy. She said she'd wait for more information and stay at home. I recall grabbing Teddy from his bed knowing he'd want him. Teddy always went to the hospital. I also remember that when I went into the bathroom and looked into the mirror it hit me that he had been with Erin and all I could think of was what if something had happened to Erin too. She had that beautiful little boy. She was his momma and he needed her.

I don't know why I wasn't in a panic. Maybe it was so I could get to the hospital safely. It didn't dawn on me that the red van was parked at the side yard and I had no idea how it had gotten there since John had it with him. We got in it and drove the forty-five minute distance.

We took the exit and then guessed our way there following the blue "H" signs. We pulled to the side of the semi-urban street to ask a young man for directions and he said he'd be glad to show us and asked if we'd mind giving him a lift in that direction. We didn't hesitate. Who knows, he could have been a serial killer! We got there and he gave us words of encouragement then went on his way. I don't remember parking or going into the hospital. I just remember things suddenly got surreal and cold and I told somebody at a window my name and that I was told by police to come here about my son John Van Horn. It was weird, I thought, that they were kind of expecting me. They told us to wait and someone would be right out. An older heavy-set guy came through a set of doors, verified who I was, I introduced Ethan, then ushered us through some doors into a hallway that seemed desolate. He proceeded to tell us that John had "jumped out of the window of a moving car and had severe head trauma". I just recall being puzzled and stunned and staring and saying, "what?" I hardly remember what Ethan did but I think it was pretty much the same.

He went on to tell us he had been life-flighted there but had minimal brain activity. I remember sliding my back down the wall and coming to rest with my bottom on the floor, trying to process it and thinking in my head, 'ok, we'll manage this, I'll take care of him for the rest of his life like Christopher Reeve, I'm his Mama.' Then strangely the thought popped into my head that he might never play the piano again and how sad that quietness would be and frustrating it would be for him. The man told us they still had him in the trauma unit and were cleaning him up and moving him to ICU so we could see him. I don't think we, at least I understood fully. We both cried. They put us in a waiting room for about half an hour.

When we got up stairs it was kind of like the ICU floors in the movies but smaller. Someone new came with us and warned us that it might be frightening. No doubt. He was on lots of machines, his head was thickly wrapped in bandages, he was on a respirator and IV's and warming blankets. He had little cuts on his hands and scrapes on his knees, but that was about it for visible injuries. I believe this is when it became completely real to Ethan and the tears began to be heavy.

Brad Parker > John Van Horn
August 8 at 9:44 pm

Hey bro, just wanted to take the time to let you know that today you had an unbelievable amount of support. So many people care about you and love you man, and we all miss you terribly. Your life is gonna be celebrated for a long time coming, and we know your spirit will live on forever in anything any of us do. Why you were taken from us so soon, we won't know, but we know clearly there's greater plans in store for you. I can't wait to pass on the many tales of John Van Horn and the crazy antics we lived through together. I will never forget the imprint you've left on my life and I'm sure everyone you've encountered feels the same. You're one of the greatest people I've ever had the pleasure of sharing life with and I wish I had shared that with you more. Please rest easy my brother, and I hope we will meet again in the future. It's never a goodbye but an until next time. Love you man.

The doctor approached us and explained the brevity of it all. John currently had the simplest form of brain function, a reflex really, breathing, which he explained was almost a reactionary function. All of his other brain activity had ceased. He was doing nothing else on his own. Everything else we saw was keeping John alive. The doctor explained, as kindly as he could that when John chose to stop breathing on his own, he would be gone. He also said that John's driver's license indicated he is and organ donor and wanted to know if we wished to honor that. I looked and Ethan and we nodded in agreement. He went on to say that if there was anyone else who would want to see him they needed to be called quickly. I said he had a sister who is 18. He said to get a hold of her. I must have looked confused because he added that it could be a matter of hours. That may have been when I realized he wasn't coming home.

I tried to reach Evy on her phone and at the house and got no answer at either so I called Bryan, but he didn't answer so I called his home phone and finally got someone. I explained to Bryan's dad what was going on and so Bryan and his mom, Paula went to the house and explained to Evy what was happening and then drove her to the hospital to be with us. You could see the heartbreak on her face as she walked in. We all cried together.

Then Ethan reminded me that we needed to call his dad. I used his phone. He was in California on vacation with his girlfriend at the time. When he answered I tried to explain that John had been in an accident, was in ICU but was not going to make it. He became very angry and began yelling at me. I repeated that his son was a short time away from death and if he wanted to see him he only had a small window, told him where he was and hung up. He called back minutes later screaming how it was all my fault, I was a horrible mother and had been the reason John was going to die. Paula could hear the entire conversation from across the room and motioned for me to just hang up, so I did. I then just broke into tears and she hugged me for what seemed like forever. I was very grateful for her kindness and support. He never came to the hospital.

Monday August 3 at about 11:30am John coded. He went into cardiac arrest. We were sitting in the hallway and the medical personnel rushed out to double check and make sure we wanted to let him be a donor or let him go. I was very confused. I said yes to being a donor. So a group of people ran into the room and revived him and then it was explained to me that if we had not decided to let him be donor then he would have left us right then and that would have been the end but they revived him. We were assured that they would take good care of him until all the organ recipients were in place and we could go home. I knew I couldn't leave. I was there when he entered this world. I would be there when he left it.

The kids decided that they would say their goodbyes and go home together. Paula would take them for me. Paula and Bryan said their goodbyes and then Evelyn and Ethan each took private time of their own. Evelyn wrote a small note to her brother and placed it in his curled hand and asked the staff to please not take it out and they didn't. I made sure it stayed there even when they wheeled him too the surgical unit. I've never asked her what it said.

One of the doctors or nurses explained to me a little more. Because John still had the breathing response on his own this apparently meant that all of his healthy organs would be viable if he "chose" to stop breathing on his own. When his breathing stopped on it's own they call time of death. If something else was the case then only kidneys were usable. They had set in motion the process of matching recipients, which I had no idea was a complicated as it was. You see some people are waiting for multiple organs so they want to match those people first and if that falls through then you go on to a separate recipient. So they've been trying to gather people together and they have to go to their respective hospitals and their surgeons come to John's hospital to do the surgery to get the organ they each needed, go home and transplant it into their patient. The OR for John took over five hours to prepare, but you can't prepare it until you have everybody matched and in place!

Meanwhile, representatives from Center for Organ Recovery and Education, CORE, our area's organ team has come and met with me, asked 28,000 questions, thanked me profusely and had me pick a poem and give them a photo of John for a small card, in packs of 100, that will be provided for us to give people at the funeral and elsewhere noting him as a hero for being a donor. They did many follow-up things as well, including letting us know a bit about the recipients and allowing us to write a letter to be sent to them telling a bit about John. We also learned about how his tissues have helped research. I made a quilt block representing John for their annual quilt of donors from 2015 and they do so much more.

I think I finally dozed off for about forty-five minutes leaning at the side of the bed holding his hand. I woke up with a start and all of a sudden realized it was reality. I remember starting to cry and repeating no, no, no over and over and a nurse came to comfort me. This new hell was my life. At some point during that morning I had to call both of my parents, not something anyone wants to tell a grandparent. I called my mom first and she asked if she should come and I told her no, she didn't want to see Johnny this way, that I'd tell her when it was over. She offered to call my brother for me. I thanked her for that. The harder call was my dad. Not only was it harder to explain to my dad, but also this day was his 75th birthday. When you answer the phone expecting a happy birthday call and get probably one of the worst calls you could imagine, how do you ever celebrate your birthday again? He really hasn't.

Erin and Brian stopped in to see him and Brian couldn't even look me in the eye but just began to cry and apologize. I hugged him and told him it wasn't his fault, that he had done everything he could and to not blame himself. He had a very hard time believing that I didn't hate him. I couldn't. He didn't push my son. He was trying to get him home to me and he would have to live with this for the rest of his life too. Erin just cried and apologized too and looked over at John and said, "at least he's going to pull through". I didn't know they hadn't been told. I had to say, "No, he's not, I'm so sorry". Then everyone just broke and I had to explain it all again. They stayed as long as they could manage, and then said their good byes.

The coroner came in to tell me that they would send a blood sample away to see what was in John's system but it could take up to Six months. The accident occurred in Centre County but the hospital is in Blair County so it would go through that county and they are very backed up. Six months, that's unbelieveable. He said an autopsy wasn't necessary because cause of death was clear. He gave me his card and condolences.

The people of the ICU were incredible people. Everybody is quick to complain about experiences, especially in healthcare, but people need to be praised. I wrote a letter to them and I hope they got it. The men and women that took care of my Johnny were special people. When they came into the room they talked to him and smoothed his covers. They were gentle with him and when they treated him this way it touched my heart. They were kind to me by being kind to him. It said to me that it didn't matter to them how he came to be there and they knew he wasn't going home but they talked to him as if he could be. They didn't assume he couldn't hear them. They took the time to look at a picture of him "before he was all wrapped up" and listen to me tell them that he was a classical pianist and that he played bass in a band. They brought me drinks and a basket of food, warm blankets and assured me it was okay to walk away for five minutes because they'd watch him for me even though he had Teddy to hold. These people were angles to me while I was alone with him.

I got a phone call from my friend Julia at some point telling me she was going to come right after work around four. I told her she didn't need to, that it was okay, but she insisted she didn't want me to be alone. I met her at the elevator when she arrived and asked her if she had ever seen anybody in really bad shape and when she said no I made her promise that if it was too much for her she would go. She never left our sides until they took him into the final surgery.

I remember walking into his room together and feeling her arm around my shoulder and hearing her comforting voice. Julia is a certified Elementary school teacher but she would have been an amazing nurse. Everything was explained to her and she tried to digest it. The sorrow on her face showed me that her heart was almost as heavy as if this was her own son lying in front of her. She had watched this young man grow up in her home too, playing with her Thomas, being foolish boys, carefree teenagers and starting to become responsible men. I know scenes of his childhood played through her mind like the old VHS movies our kids were raised watching.

His eyes wouldn't close all the way because of the swelling so I could barely see a bit of his beautiful blue peeking out, but knowing he couldn't see me back was breaking me. They continued to keep wrapping his head because of blood loss. They layered on top of the existing bandage so we tried to make light and say he was starting to look like a Cone head because of the way it was starting to wrap. His extremities were on the cold side and the nurse explained that they were keeping his core temperature warmer to keep his organs functioning correctly. He hated being cold recently. To look at his arms and legs there were very few cuts and scrapes and no apparent bruises. The first doctor had assured us that when John hit his head he had gone quickly unconscious and felt no pain. "He didn't suffer". They like to tell you that. I'm sure medically they know the body and the mechanics so I do hope he was correct because he suffered enough before that.

Time stood still and flew at the same time. My pastor came and went. I barely stopped talking to John. I thanked him for so many things and much of that became the basis of the poem Thank you. I wished so much I could have petted his hair because that's what I did when my kids didn't feel well. It's what my mom did for me, but I couldn't. I couldn't even see my baby's soft, soft hair. The funeral home gave us some of his hair to keep. So I just stroked his arms. I went back and forth between apologizing for not being able to fix everything, for not being able to help him fix his brain and then telling him I didn't think it even made sense at that point and lastly I'd find myself harkening back to my darkest of times and leaning on his chest and telling him I understood if he felt he had to go. I knew no one else would ever understand my saying that but him. No matter what got him in that bed he was my son and I loved him unconditionally and I would have switched places with him. I still would at any given moment. That's what a mom does.

I'm not sure of the conversations Julia and I had, I just know she was there and that's all that mattered. She chatted with John too and talked about things he had done in years past. Sometime in the afternoon I got up and quietly went to the sink in the corner of the room and took the washcloth and a bit of soap and one at a time I washed his feet. Jesus washed the disciples feet and said, "ye also should do as I have done to you" and it symbolizes humility and service. I'm not sure why I felt compelled to do this but I did and I wept. I felt that he was ready now and could go. Around

5:40 pm John stopped his breathing reflex on his own. It was as if he knew he had to so all of his organs could help others. Now everything, including the respirator was animating his body. But I stayed. It was all a matter of waiting for recipients and surgeons.

That night there was a terrible thunderstorm with loud thunder and vibrant lightening. I had told my friend Luke, who had taken welding with me and had come to know John, about what happened. He had become protective of our family during that school year. He later told me that during the storm he was calling to John and saying, "yeah man, I know it's you talking to us". He said it was Johnny's way of making his last statement here on earth.

So the third of August had come and gone. I knew it was time to let the rest of the world know what happened before bits and pieces began leaking out so I posted on Social Media the words that began this book and responses began pouring in. I didn't really read anything until I got home because I wanted to spend all my moments with John. They updated us and said that everybody should be in place by mid-day and that's when they would take him in for the surgery. I was beginning to realize I'd have to let him go. Every now and then I'd start to panic. How could I let him go?

The time did come. They came to me and said everything was in place and they would be taking him down to the surgical suite in just a few minutes and that I should say my goodbyes. I was just barely getting adjusted to his being in the hospital, that he had "gotten hurt…really badly", now I have to say goodbye? I know he was technically gone since yesterday but his being was still in front of me. I can't just let them roll him away and wave like he's headed off on an Alaskan cruise because he's not coming back, ever. How do you say goodbye to a piece of your heart, a piece of yourself. I feel now, as I write this like I just let them but I know I didn't. He was gone. Some of his body had other things to do now. He could go on being the giver he always was and live on somehow. Still, how do you just let go of your first born, the one who made you "mama"?

I kissed him one last time and so did Teddy. I told him how much I loved him and would miss him. Through tears I made them promise not to lose the note his sister had given him and make sure it went to the funeral home. I held his hand until the last possible second. I wanted to scream, "Please don't go Johnny"! You read in biblical stories where people tear their clothing because of grief and sorrow, it makes perfect sense to me now. I felt like tearing my sweatshirt and then my own skin because crying wasn't enough to release the pain that my heart felt, but you have to show restraint. Sally field demonstrates this feeling beautifully in the graveside scene in Steel Magnolias when she loses composure expressing her grief and talks about her daughter she just buried then quickly tries to pull herself together to make it look like she is in control. You do this so often at first and then you almost begin living like this, trying to convince people you have it together when slightly under the surface you are just shy of a boil over.

If I could have expelled all the breath from my lungs that day and fallen on to the floor like a limp, empty balloon I would have but I couldn't push the air from my chest no matter how hard I tried. I wanted to go with him so desperately, but somehow logic overruled and I knew he couldn't stay and I couldn't go so I watched through pained and tear-filled burning eyes as my son left my sight and physical life forever. Part of me died as I willed myself to walk away. A hole developed within my heart that can never be repaired and ever so slowly grows larger with each realization of things that will now never be because of his absence.

Chapter 14

The After

With Julia by my side I exited the hospital and she lead me to my van. She hugged me one last time, offered to drive me home and have her husband, Scott, bring me back later for my van but I declined explaining I didn't want to have to go back there. She understood, as she always did. I was carrying all that I had left of my son from that night in a clear plastic hospital bag not unlike those I had filled so many times before from the behavioral health unit at our own hospital. It held the shorts they had cut from his body at the scene, his belt, and his wallet. I held in my arms his Teddy. For years we said that Teddy was always awake to watch over Johnny and I looked at him now and through tears I said, " You can go to sleep now Teddy".

I remember opening the sliding door of the van and seeing John's, now pink, red Van's sneakers on the floor. He must have left them in the van while playing in the hose Sunday night. It instantly brought more tears. To this day I have left those sneakers on the porch outside of my kitchen door, among everyone else's, since taking them out of the van and I cannot get rid of them. In my mind I leave them out so he will have shoes in case he comes back. I get into the driver's seat and then put Teddy in the front passenger seat and strap him in just to have something to be light about. It is an incredibly bright and sunny day. I hate it.

I make it home somehow and when I pull into the driveway I find Ethan and Evelyn sitting in the grass in the side yard. We often all did this and frequently all the cats would join us. This time was different. I just went over and joined them. No words were exchanged. I think we all just sat there, numb and dazed and then we cried. I think Daniel arrived soon after and the crying continued.

I can't begin to tell which days were which but I was keeping it together pretty well at first. Food began to arrive, as if anyone wanted to eat! I don't remember when my Mom got there but she came ahead of her husband and my dad. Patty, Daniel's mom, was there and I just remember wandering the house the night it happened, the night I broke. You see I had gone shopping Sunday afternoon and had texted John to see if he wanted watermelon, an absolute favorite of his. I've kept the text. He said he would and I got one. It was sitting on the countertop just behind the kitchen door a bit out of sight. I walked into the kitchen and caught a glimpse of that darn watermelon and that's when I broke.

I suddenly realized that John would never get to eat that watermelon and I grabbed it and fell to the floor crying so hard I couldn't breathe. I'm sure I was completely incoherent and I know this is the first my kids saw me lose it like this and I expect it scared them or maybe it made them feel better. I don't know. I didn't want that watermelon ever to be cut or eaten. I wish I could have preserved it like people bronze baby shoes. When I finally came through that I felt like I needed to be led around like a child for a while, but that was "when I broke". I think I had enough safe people nearby that I could allow myself to do that. As crazy as it sounds to say sometimes I want to go back to the first days, not because I want to re-live it, but because everyone would understand and let me walk around in a daze again and not function and they'd be okay with it. I'll say to Evelyn when we know someone who looses a child and they are holding it together well, "they didn't see their watermelon yet". She knows exactly what I mean.

Funeral arrangers are incredible and I am grateful for what they do. Daniel and Patty went with me to make the arrangements. It wasn't something either of the kids was ready to do and John's dad was still out of town but, the funeral home planner went to his home when he was available to go through every detail and he signed that he was in agreement with the plans, including cremation, which was John's wish.

They were very encouraging about having his favorite music playing during the visitation and that we should be sure to have lots of pictures to showcase his life and include as many personal belongings as we wished. Ethan spent many hours compiling a CD of music from punk to classical, to metal and even some of their band to play that morning. Because of John's great sense of humor it was agreed upon that we use a cookie jar his Grammy (my mom) had gotten him years earlier that was a shark, which when you lifted his mouth the buh, buh, buh, buh, Jaws theme noise plays as John's urn. John in his shark now grace the top of our piano, the most appropriate spot in our house. His brother and sister helped pick out things like his bass, skateboard, Teddy and other things to represent him at the visitation. The picture boards were great and the service itself was touching. I had them include a quote from Calvin and Hobbes that he currently had on his Social Media wall; "If people sat outside and looked at the stars each night I bet they would live a lot differently". I also had a quote read from a Robin Williams movie because we did a lot of talking about his passing and I thought it summed up John well: "Please don't worry so much. Because in the end, none of us have very long on this earth. Life is fleeting. And if you're ever distressed, cast your eyes to the summer sky when the stars are strung across the velvety night. And when a shooting star streaks through the blackness, turning night into day...make a wish and think of me. Make your life spectacular. I know I did."

We tried to put a bit of humor in his obituary and in among information about him and his accomplishments and things he liked I added that he never put away his laundry. The last line was a quote from "It's a Wonderful Life" and I thought it appropriate because of how he doubted himself and thought he failed at so much: "No man is a failure who has friends". I hope he knows how true that is.

It was a lovely service and we had a gathering at our home following. So many people came to celebrate his life and remember the times they had with him. We had a bonfire, food, kids just hanging out feeling comforted. They were welcome to stay and they knew that. I woke up on Sunday morning to find several of them sleeping on the porch just because they couldn't bring themselves to leave and that was okay. They weren't ready to let go.

After everything passed with the funeral we began to try to figure out how to live. I had to proceed with a scheduled tonsillectomy on the following Monday. At 48 years old this was a pretty major surgery so my mom stayed behind for a few days and sent her husband and my dad back home. Being in a hospital so soon after the days in the ICU was very emotionally difficult but I got through it and came out of surgery fine but pretty beat. By the end of the week, although weak I explained to Mom that we needed to figure out how to do this by ourselves and she headed back to Pittsburgh leaving behind lots of love and strict instructions to call if we needed help. I was back in a job search since I had just graduated in June and figured if I couldn't find a position in my new welding field I'd go back to day to day subbing and reactivated my status with the local district. I had passed the state exam to be a life insurance agent and had a position with a local firm but seeing that it would require a great deal of daily travel and average 10 hours a day and sometimes six days a week I spoke to them and bowed out of the position. As much as I wanted to move forward bills were coming in. It was a good five weeks before I could eat real food again, so between the June hospital stay for the throat abscess that left me at 99 pounds, losing my appetite after John and the surgery immediately following I was not in the best shape but I did my best to press on.

The end of August came and so did the start of school. I took sub jobs and realized I was in no shape mentally to be actively job hunting so stayed where I was. CPI asked me to be on their sub list since I had subbed while I was a student. I gladly did. The atmosphere is different there. It has a family feeling and they knew my situation so it was comfortable being there. If I was low or weepy no one questioned. Shortly into the school year an instructional assistant position was advertised there for collision repair, where Evelyn returned as an adult student for a year, and automotive programs so I applied. After the interview process I heard back and was hired by late October. I've been with CPI ever since in one capacity or another. It depends on the year and enrollment and where I can help the most. It has been a blessing to be there. They will always be another family to me.

It is very hard to decide what to do with the belongings of someone you lose. John was a very giving person so when we went through his clothing we kept only the items that were of personal, sentimental value to any of us. The rest we passed on to friends or organizations. His sister and I discussed and chose to give his beloved car to Ethan. She has since completely restored it for him (did it during her adult year at CPI). John really didn't have much "stuff". We kept all his instruments, most of which are in the dining room and are sometimes played. Teddy got a new button down shirt made out of a favorite pair or John's shorts and takes turns "living" with me and Ethan. He had a huge tee shirt collection and his brother and sister chose between them and I made both of them a cozy quilt out of them.

Realizing how much they meant I gathered enough things to make one for myself that included a karate uniform top and pajama pants to get enough items. I couldn't just get rid of things on his dresser so I carefully collected them and stored them in two decorated boxes I got at half-price at a craft store. One says, "All who wander are not lost", which I think speaks clearly about John. I feel close to him on days that I wear his flannels. Every person has to make their own choices about things like that but I like to keep his things in view rather than hiding them away. On the second Christmas I gave Ethan and Evelyn each a gift of a large pendant of blown glass. It has a small bit of John's ashes swirled among beautiful red and clear glass. I have a smaller version of my own. The work is outstanding and shines wonderfully in the light.

In 2016 we decided to create the "John Van Horn Memorial Award and Gift" to be presented to an adult student in the precision machine class at CPI so that someone with his characteristics could be recognized. The guidelines were to be as follows: the student need not be the top student but one who has a great interest in learning, someone who shows kindness to others, has a love of life and a childlike spirit. The first year the recipient had been in class with him the year before so that was even more meaningful.

As the years go by it doesn't get any easier as some people assure you it will. It just gets different. You learn different ways to cope, ways to remember and celebrate him. I take a lot of cues from the kids on how to deal with holidays and such. We have changed traditions and meals on Easter and Christmas, but still watch our favorite movies. On his 25th birthday Ethan made 23 origami cranes and Evy and I each made one. We then went to the creek and floated them down and wished him a happy birthday. I think each year is going to be different. You have to go with how you are feeling. Sometimes it's just quiet. I find it very hard to get to know new people because they didn't know John. I do feel more withdrawn sometimes because it is safer in my mind. I wish people wouldn't avoid the subject of John because it makes me feel like they want to pretend he didn't exist and that hurts more than being afraid to be sad, but John doesn't make me sad, not having him here does and those are two very different things. If we focus only on the bad then there is no reason to get up, don't you think?

The question of faith has come up after losing John. It hasn't happened to me too frequently because my closest friends are strong believers in Jesus Christ. There is always the question of whether or not I was/am mad at God. No, it is hard to go on in my life without my son but I know that because of God and His son Jesus and my belief and because John put his trust in him years ago I will see him again. I don't believe God took my son. I see it more as a reaching out and catching him when he needed to be caught. It may sound pure and simple, but it is. I know this has made many people, especially young people, even family members, question their faith but I hope that they will come to reconcile their feelings and again find their faith because it will get them through. Yes there are days that I wonder how I will continue another 25 or more years without John but on good days I remember I have far more days beyond that with him than without him. It's the bad days that take the most faith and strength.

The pain goes far beyond myself. I look at my children and see a bit of emptiness in their eyes. Everyone remembers me as the mom who lost her son but few remember that they lost their brother. They don't know my pain and I can't even begin to understand theirs. My future changed, yes, but not the way theirs has. They have so many decades ahead that have been altered because of their loss. Their wedding parties won't be the same. That silly song he and Evy planned as she exited the church won't happen now. Where will crazy Uncle Johnny be? There will be forever a brother missing at holidays to add to stories of "hey, remember when we…". Who will draw penises on the snow covered cars to make everyone laugh now? It's as though their past, present and futures have all changed at once. There are so many support groups for parents but nothing it seems for siblings, especially in their late teens and twenties. They are the "forgotten mourners", do people think because they are young they will bounce back? My heart breaks for them now too. People mean well and Evy says people say at Christmas, "holidays must be hard"' she said just once she wants to respond' NO, they're great, what do you think???" but she is too polite.

I try to make something good out of something awful as much as I can. I speak to students at school who are of driving age and urge them to become organ donors. I speak to the nursing classes about the care that they give to not only the patients but to the families. I speak to the first responder students and express to them that whenever they respond to a call they must not judge the circumstance but realize that the patient is someone's brother, son, friend, teammate and they are needed at home so do their best. I advocate for mental health when I can, I reach out to hurting students and try to make sure people understand. We need to understand.

Erin now works in a behavioral health setting and finds it frustrating at times when other people lack the patience or compassion needed for the job. Sometimes they can't figure out how she does it and she stated to me that she just looks at the patients and thinks to herself that any one of them could be someone's "John". We need more people like her.

There is no correct response to the loss of a child and no proper amount of time to grieve. As a matter of fact I don't think any parent ever stops grieving, in their own way and that grief looks very different from person to person. No parent should ever be judged by the way they choose to manage their grief. I've been told that I've been through a lot of struggles and even before I began to reestablish my world without John I was talking with Evelyn and said I've always thought that some people are meant to have hard lives, not as punishment, but so that they can make it through and be a good example of perseverance. That way someday people may look to them and be encouraged to do the same.

An easy life doesn't let you rely on family, friends, creativity, inner strength or God. It doesn't allow you to grow to your full potential and want to become better. It doesn't make you appreciate all of the little things you have or the big ones. Sometimes it is during the hardest times that you notice the most beauty because you wonder if you will make it through to ever see beauty again.

Sarah Bumgarner
August 4 at 1:14pm

It was good to know you John, even for just a little while. Rest in Peace.

Chapter 15

Closure...Doesn't Exist

A bit more than six months after John's death and after many calls to the coroner's office I finally got the results of the toxicology report. As I sat in the hallway outside of the Auto Tech classroom where I was assisting, my head was spinning. I wrote down what the man said so I didn't forget. He said John's blood contained legal levels of alcohol and there was OxyCodone, and traces of Klonopin, so there was nothing illegal in his system. That made me feel a little bit better, I don't know why. He had been prescribed the OxyCodone for an ankle injury several months back and he had probably just kept them and he had gotten a hold of Klonopin before. After talking to several medical professionals about drug/alcohol interactions, researching and listening to the story again about his behavior being so very unlike himself, many of us truly believe he didn't comprehend that the car was moving when he got out. No one will ever know for sure and it is something many will never agree on and it is a terrible memory that the people who were with him have to live with. We must remember they could not have anticipated all of his actions. Because of quick thinking he was life-flighted to a trauma center and was able to save many lives and for that a multitude of people are grateful.

Some final thoughts

Three years have passed now and I have reflected on so many aspects of my son's death, my own mortality and purpose and much more. I've struggled through the decision to even write this book fearing it would be upsetting to him but realizing in the end that he was the most honest and open person and would want very much for others to benefit from what he had experienced, both good and bad. As he said, ".I want everyone to see that this world, this life, is absolutely fuckin beautiful, and it doesn't matter who or what you are, you should do even the smallest things for everyone. I want this needless me, me, me mindset to end." If this book can cause people to reset their thinking then it will be worth it.

I believe that the way John lived his life showed God's unselfish love and that's why we were put on this earth. His time was short but the impact he made will go on long beyond those years. Yes, part of me died on August 3, 2015. Now I am choosing to re-grow a new part of me hoping to be a reflection of his best self mixed with my best self. I stop every now and again and ask myself if I'm going in the right direction and remind myself that ultimately I choose my path, as do all of us. I can choose joy, choose to find contentment in whatever job I do, and find purpose wherever I am. I must be deliberate. There are days of sadness but that doesn't mean I've failed at my task. There are days of joy and laughter and that does not mean I no longer miss my son. There is a balance. One year on John's birthday Ethan was playing John's bass and although he felt a great closeness to his brother he was overwhelmingly sad and wept. I tried to help by explaining that there will probably be a day where the feeling of joy and great closeness will overpower the sadness and this will be true for many things but he will have to look for it and treasure it.

I don't want anyone to be sad about John forever and I highly doubt he would either. I want the best of him and his memories to be what changes my life and the lives of others. So at his suggestion...

"Let's go outside,
It's a beautiful day,
It's a beautiful life."

Thank you Johnny

Thank you…

for never sleeping as a baby… all those extra hours I wouldn't have otherwise,

for your contagious smile,

for showing me how to feel music, not just hear it,

for teaching me patience by having to practice it,

for helping me learn more about myself through learning about you,

for always understanding me,

for helping me learn to be a mama,

for knowing my thoughts even when I couldn't express them,

for your constant encouragement,

for being hilarious,

for trying so hard and becoming yourself this last year,

for teaching me the real meaning of unconditional love,

for valuing me,

for "hanging with me",

for being the least judgmental person I've ever known,

for loving to learn,

for loving others,

for making the most of life,

for overcoming obstacles,

for your music,

for your compassion, for your honesty,

for your sincerity,

for your openness,

for your love,

for your never being too big or embarrassed to hug me in front of friends,

for your friendship,

for being goofy,

for teaching me to look at the world through new eyes.

Thank you for being my son.

Michelle, September 2015

Forlorn

The fragrance of autumn
is filling the air.
A chill each morn
with bright sun and heat each afternoon.
Crickets' songs break the solemn dinner hour.
The gray fall sky warns us.

It all begins.
Once brightly green flourishing leaves
brown and wither upon each edge.
Trees dress themselves vividly, but oh so briefly.
Flowers wilt and bud no more.
Morning dew becomes killing frost.

Songs of birds transform,
a beckoning call to escape.
Little creatures turn from frolic
to endless rush of gathering.
The final waft of warm summer air passes,
pushed aside by the crisp bite of autumn wind.

Thoughts of change fill my head.
I desperately hold
to the last leaf that clings
to its life upon the branch,
for when it falls
so will end my last summer with you.

How can I go forward
and face the changing season,
one that used to smell so strongly
of comfort and safety,
of closeness and enjoyment,
even of beginnings.

I scarcely see beyond
the darkness that is to come,

The band playing one
of their last gigs.

Enjoying time with Kayla

Posing in his ninth grade football

The Christmas he wanted to play the organ
instead of opening his presents.

Afternoon bath fun with Ethan.

John's stellar Mohawk that he shaved just
before entering CPI for precision machine.

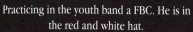

Practicing in the youth band a FBC. He is in
the red and white hat.

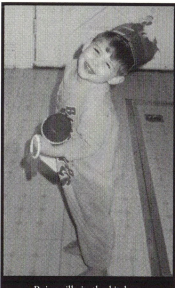

Being silly in the kitchen.

Earning a higher rank in Tan Soo Do.

Posing in precision machine class.

Napping with Grampa
(Michelle's Dad).

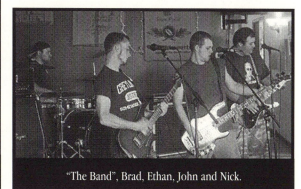

"The Band", Brad, Ethan, John and Nick.

The picture of John taken on the porch that I think looked into his soul those last days of summer.

John and Ethan at System of a Down concert in D.C. one summer.

The last Fourth of July when he tagged along with Ev.

On the front porch with Grammy (Michelle's mom) and Ethan at the Bellefonte house.

I love the intensity of this shot of him singing.

John's First Christmas.

John playing in the LHU Jazz Ensemble

A very emotional performance face.

John and Daniel in the Siamese twin
Halloween costume.

John relaxing with his best buddy Otis.

John and Ethan on
graduation night from CPI.

My typical "yard man". Always there to help and making it fun.

Relaxing with Owen cat in the field outside the rental house near Philly.

The day Bryson called him "uncle John" and then fell asleep on his back before they could play Hungry, Hungry Hippos.uniform.

John with his sister, Evelyn, on the night he, Ethan and I graduated. She had graduated with the high school students the week prior.

A great summer afternoon playing football with friends in the side yard. Bryan, Evy Ethan John and Jordan.

His high school senior picture taken on the porch swing.

Erin surprised Jon on his 23rd Birthday with cupcakes.

Jon and lil' Blue.

Photo Credits

Epilogue

Some of the most meaningful books I have read on the subject of Bipolar Illness or Manic Depressive, which I think is a more understandable and descriptive term, have been beautifully written by Kay Redfeild Jamison. Because of her honestly written material, which comes from both a medical background and from her life experiences as a manic-depressive sufferer, I can walk taller and have a greater hope for others and myself. In the epilogue contained in An Unquiet Mind she addresses the question of whether or not, given the choice, she would choose to rid herself of this affliction. So I have decided to ponder this question as well from another perspective.

If I could have taken bipolar from my son would I have done so? I believe much of who he was and the amazing young man he became rose out of his struggles. I do believe his incredible musical ability and extraordinary talent were directly related to his condition and I would not have taken that from him. I do however wish a proper medication and treatment protocol would have been discovered that would have stabilized his moods and not caused him concern about loosing artistic ability. I truly wish he would have had the time to mature further into adulthood and had the opportunity to develop the cognitive growth needed to understand certain things a young man of 23 did not yet grasp. I do so desperately wish he were here for his brother and sister to have to share the rest of their adult lives together and I truly wish there would have been time for his dad and him to come to a common ground.

Having bipolar illness is a very difficult life to live. It is an ever-changing challenge. For many, you dread constantly feeling like a burden so you never ask or stop asking for help. In our society it's even harder. I don't' believe I would take it from him because I wouldn't know him any other way and I don't believe I'd take it from myself. It's part of who we are, our weakness and also our strength. John wouldn't have truly existed as John without bipolar. It's part of what made him truly amazing and "well, at least he didn't have lava on his face".

Appendices

Information from NAMI
National Alliance for Mental Illness
www.nami.org

Bipolar disorder is a mental illness that causes dramatic shifts in a person's mood, energy and ability to think clearly. People with bipolar experience high and low moods—known as mania and depression—which differ from the typical ups-and-downs most people experience.

The average age-of-onset is about 25, but it can occur in the teens, or more uncommonly, in childhood. The condition affects men and women equally, with about 2.6% of the U.S. population diagnosed with bipolar disorder and nearly 83% of cases classified as severe.

If left untreated, bipolar disorder usually worsens. However, with a good treatment plan including psychotherapy, medications, a healthy lifestyle, a regular schedule and early identification of symptoms, many people live well with the condition.

SYMPTOMS

Symptoms and their severity can vary. A person with bipolar disorder may have distinct manic or depressed states but may also have extended periods—sometimes years—without symptoms. A person can also experience both extremes simultaneously or in rapid sequence.

Severe bipolar episodes of mania or depression may include psychotic symptoms such as hallucinations or delusions. Usually, these psychotic symptoms mirror a person's extreme mood. People with bipolar disorder who have psychotic symptoms can be wrongly diagnosed as having schizophrenia.

Mania. To be diagnosed with bipolar disorder, a person must have experienced at least one episode of mania or hypomania. Hypomania is a milder form of mania that doesn't include psychotic episodes. People with hypomania can often function well in social situations or at work. Some people with bipolar disorder will have episodes of mania or hypomania many times throughout their life; others may experience them only rarely.

Although someone with bipolar may find an elevated mood of mania appealing—especially if it occurs after depression—the "high" does not stop at a comfortable or controllable level. Moods can rapidly become more irritable, behavior more unpredictable and judgment more impaired. During periods of mania, people frequently behave impulsively, make reckless decisions and take unusual risks.

Most of the time, people in manic states are unaware of the negative consequences of their actions. With bipolar disorder, suicide is an ever-present danger because some people become suicidal even in manic states. Learning from prior episodes what kinds of behavior signals "red flags" of manic behavior can help manage the symptoms of the illness.

Depression. The lows of bipolar depression are often so debilitating that people may be unable to get out of bed. Typically, people experiencing a depressive episode have difficulty falling and staying asleep, while others sleep far more than usual. When people are depressed, even minor decisions such as what to eat for dinner can be overwhelming. They may become obsessed with feelings of loss, personal failure, guilt or helplessness; this negative thinking can lead to thoughts of suicide.

The depressive symptoms that obstruct a person's ability to function must be present nearly every day for a period of at least two weeks for a diagnosis. Depression associated with bipolar disorder may be more difficult to treat and require a customized treatment plan.

CAUSES

Scientists have not yet discovered a single cause of bipolar disorder. Currently, they believe several factors may contribute, including:

- **Genetics.** The chances of developing bipolar disorder are increased if a child's parents or siblings have the disorder. But the role of genetics is not absolute: A child from a family with a history of bipolar disorder may never develop the disorder. Studies of identical twins have found that, even if one twin develops the disorder, the other may not.

- **Stress.** A stressful event such as a death in the family, an illness, a difficult relationship, divorce or financial problems can trigger a manic or depressive episode. Thus, a person's handling of stress may also play a role in the development of the illness.

- **Brain structure and function.** Brain scans cannot diagnose bipolar disorder, yet researchers have identified subtle differences in the average size or activation of some brain structures in people with bipolar disorder.

DIAGNOSIS

To diagnose bipolar disorder, a doctor may perform a physical examination, conduct an interview and order lab tests. While bipolar disorder cannot be seen on a blood test or body scan, these tests can help rule out other illnesses that can resemble the disorder, such as hyperthyroidism. If no other illnesses (or medicines such as steroids) are causing the symptoms, the doctor may recommend mental health care.

To be diagnosed with bipolar disorder, a person must have experienced at least one episode of mania or hypomania. Mental health care professionals use the Diagnostic and Statistical Manual of Mental Disorders (DSM) to diagnose the "type" of bipolar disorder a person may be experiencing. To determine what type of bipolar disorder a person has, mental health care professionals assess the pattern of symptoms and how impaired the person is during their most severe episodes.
Four Types of Bipolar Disorder

1. **Bipolar I Disorder** is an illness in which people have experienced one or more episodes of mania. Most people diagnosed with bipolar I will have episodes of both mania and depression, though an episode of depression is not necessary for a diagnosis. To be diagnosed with bipolar I, a person's manic episodes must last at least seven days or be so severe that hospitalization is required.

2. **Bipolar II Disorder** is a subset of bipolar disorder in which people experience depressive episodes shifting back and forth with hypo manic episodes, but never a "full" manic episode.

3. **Cyclothymic Disorder or Cyclothymia** is a chronically unstable mood state in which people experience hypomania and mild depression for at least two years. People with cyclothymia may have brief periods of normal mood, but these periods last less than eight weeks.

4. **Bipolar Disorder,** "other specified" and "unspecified" is when a person does not meet the criteria for bipolar I, II or cyclothymia but has still experienced periods of clinically significant abnormal mood elevation.

TREATMENT

Bipolar disorder is treated and managed in several ways:

- **Psychotherapy**, such as cognitive behavioral therapy and family-focused therapy.

- **Medications,** such as mood stabilizers, antipsychotic medications and, to a lesser extent, antidepressants.

- **Self-management strategies,** like education and recognition of an episode's early symptoms.

- **Complementary health approaches,** such as aerobic exercise meditation, faith and prayer can support, but not replace, treatment.

The largest research project to assess what treatment methods work for people with bipolar disorder is the Systematic Treatment Enhancement for Bipolar Disorder, otherwise known as Step-BD. Step-BD followed over 4,000 people diagnosed with bipolar disorder over time with different treatments.

RELATED CONDITIONS

People with bipolar disorder can also experience:

- Anxiety
- Attention-deficit hyperactivity disorder (ADHD)
- Posttraumatic stress disorder (PTSD)
- Substance use disorders/dual diagnosis

People with bipolar disorder and psychotic symptoms can be wrongly diagnosed with schizophrenia. Bipolar disorder can be also misdiagnosed as Borderline Personality Disorder (BPD).

These other illnesses and misdiagnoses can make it hard to treat bipolar disorder. For example, the antidepressants used to treat OCD and the stimulants used to treat ADHD may worsen symptoms of bipolar disorder and may even trigger a manic episode. If you have more than one condition (called co-occurring disorders), be sure to get a treatment plan that works for you.

Information from:
National Institute of Mental Health
www.nimh.nih.gov

BIPOLAR DISORDER OVERVIEW

Bipolar disorder, also known as manic-depressive illness, is a brain disorder that causes unusual shifts in mood, energy, activity levels, and the ability to carry out day-to-day tasks.

There are four basic types of bipolar disorder; all of them involve clear changes in mood, energy, and activity levels. These moods range from periods of extremely "up," elated, and energized behavior (known as manic episodes) to very sad, "down," or hopeless periods (known as depressive episodes). Less severe manic periods are known as hypomanic episodes.

- **Bipolar I Disorder**— defined by manic episodes that last at least 7 days, or by manic symptoms that are so severe that the person needs immediate hospital care. Usually, depressive episodes occur as well, typically lasting at least 2 weeks. Episodes of depression with mixed features (having depression and manic symptoms at the same time) are also possible.

- **Bipolar II Disorder**— defined by a pattern of depressive episodes and hypomanic episodes, but not the full-blown manic episodes described above.

- **Cyclothymic Disorder** (also called cyclothymia)— defined by numerous periods of hypomanic symptoms as well numerous periods of depressive symptoms lasting for at least 2 years (1 year in children and adolescents). However, the symptoms do not meet the diagnostic requirements for a hypomanic episode and a depressive episode.

- **Other Specified and Unspecified Bipolar and Related Disorders**— defined by bipolar disorder symptoms that do not match the three categories listed above.

SIGNS AND SYMPTOMS

People with bipolar disorder experience periods of unusually intense emotion, changes in sleep patterns and activity levels, and unusual behaviors. These distinct periods are called "mood episodes." Mood episodes are drastically different from the moods and behaviors that are typical for the person. Extreme changes in energy, activity, and sleep go along with mood episodes.

People having a manic episode may:

- Feel very "up," "high," or elated
- Have a lot of energy
- Have increased activity levels
- Feel "jumpy" or "wired"
- Have trouble sleeping
- Become more active than usual
- Talk really fast about a lot of different things
- Be agitated, irritable, or "touchy"
- Feel like their thoughts are going very fast
- Think they can do a lot of things at once
- Do risky things, like spend a lot of money or have reckless sex

People having a depressive episode may:

- Feel very sad, down, empty, or hopeless
- Have very little energy
- Have decreased activity levels
- Have trouble sleeping, they may sleep too little or too much
- Feel like they can't enjoy anything
- Feel worried and empty
- Have trouble concentrating
- Forget things a lot
- Eat too much or too little
- Feel tired or "slowed down"
- Think about death or suicide

Sometimes a mood episode includes symptoms of both manic and depressive symptoms. This is called an episode with mixed features. People experiencing an episode with mixed features may feel very sad, empty, or hopeless, while at the same time feeling extremely energized.

Bipolar disorder can be present even when mood swings are less extreme. For example, some people with bipolar disorder experience hypomania, a less severe form of mania. During a hypomanic episode, an individual may feel very good, be highly productive, and function well. The person may not feel that anything is wrong, but family and friends may recognize the mood swings and/or changes in activity levels as possible bipolar disorder. Without proper treatment, people with hypomania may develop severe mania or depression.

DIAGNOSIS

Proper diagnosis and treatment help people with bipolar disorder lead healthy and productive lives. Talking with a doctor or other licensed mental health professional is the first step for anyone who thinks he or she may have bipolar disorder. The doctor can complete a physical exam to rule out other conditions. If the problems are not caused by other illnesses, the doctor may conduct a mental health evaluation or provide a referral to a trained mental health professional, such as a psychiatrist, who is experienced in diagnosing and treating bipolar disorder.

Note for Health Care Providers: People with bipolar disorder are more likely to seek help when they are depressed than when experiencing mania or hypomania. Therefore, a careful medical history is needed to ensure that bipolar disorder is not mistakenly diagnosed as major depression. Unlike people with bipolar disorder, people who have depression only (also called unipolar depression) do not experience mania. They may, however, experience some manic symptoms at the same time, which is also known as major depressive disorder with mixed features.

BIPOLAR DISORDER AND OTHER ILLNESSES

Some bipolar disorder symptoms are similar to other illnesses, which can make it hard for a doctor to make a diagnosis. In addition, many people have bipolar disorder along with another illness such as anxiety disorder, substance abuse, or an eating disorder. People with bipolar disorder are also at higher risk for thyroid disease, migraine headaches, heart disease, diabetes, obesity, and other physical illnesses.

Psychosis: Sometimes, a person with severe episodes of mania or depression also has psychotic symptoms, such as hallucinations or delusions. The psychotic symptoms tend to match the person's extreme mood. For example:

- Someone having psychotic symptoms during a manic episode may believe she is famous, has a lot of money, or has special powers.

- Someone having psychotic symptoms during a depressive episode may believe he is ruined and penniless, or that he has committed a crime.

As a result, people with bipolar disorder who also have psychotic symptoms are sometimes misdiagnosed with schizophrenia.

Anxiety and ADHD: Anxiety disorders and attention-deficit hyperactivity disorder (ADHD) are often diagnosed among people with bipolar disorder.

Substance Abuse: People with bipolar disorder may also misuse alcohol or drugs, have relationship problems, or perform poorly in school or at work. Family, friends and people experiencing symptoms may not recognize these problems as signs of a major mental illness such as bipolar disorder.

RISK FACTORS

Scientists are studying the possible causes of bipolar disorder. Most agree that there is no single cause. Instead, it is likely that many factors contribute to the illness or increase risk.

Brain Structure and Functioning: Some studies show how the brains of people with bipolar disorder may differ from the brains of healthy people or people with other mental disorders. Learning more about these differences, along with new information from genetic studies, helps scientists better understand bipolar disorder and predict which types of treatment will work most effectively.

Genetics: Some research suggests that people with certain genes are more likely to develop bipolar disorder than others. But genes are not the only risk factor for bipolar disorder. Studies of identical twins have shown that even if one twin develops bipolar disorder, the other twin does not always develop the disorder, despite the fact that identical twins share all of the same genes.

Family History: Bipolar disorder tends to run in families. Children with a parent or sibling who has bipolar disorder are much more likely to develop the illness, compared with children who do not have a family history of the disorder. However, it is important to note that most people with a family history of bipolar disorder will not develop the illness.

TREATMENTS AND THERAPIES

Treatment helps many people—even those with the most severe forms of bipolar disorder—gain better control of their mood swings and other bipolar symptoms. An effective treatment plan usually includes a combination of medication and psychotherapy (also called "talk therapy"). Bipolar disorder is a lifelong illness. Episodes of mania and depression typically come back over time. Between episodes, many people with bipolar disorder are free of mood changes, but some people may have lingering symptoms. Long-term, continuous treatment helps to control these symptoms.

MEDICATIONS

Different types of medications can help control symptoms of bipolar disorder. An individual may need to try several different medications before finding ones that work best.

Medications generally used to treat bipolar disorder include:

- Mood stabilizers
- Atypical antipsychotics
- Antidepressants

Anyone taking a medication should:

- Talk with a doctor or a pharmacist to understand the risks and benefits of the medication
- Report any concerns about side effects to a doctor right away. The doctor may need to change the dose or try a different medication.
- Avoid stopping a medication without talking to a doctor first. Suddenly stopping a medication may lead to "rebound" or worsening of bipolar disorder symptoms. Other uncomfortable or potentially dangerous withdrawal effects are also possible.
- Report serious side effects to the U.S. Food and Drug Administration (FDA) MedWatch Adverse Event Reporting program online at http://www.fda.gov/Safety/MedWatch or by phone at 1-800-332-1088. Clients and doctors may send reports.

For basic information about medications, visit the NIMH Mental Health Medications webpage. For the most up-to-date information on medications, side effects, and warnings, visit the FDA website.

PSYCHOTHERAPY

When done in combination with medication, psychotherapy (also called "talk therapy") can be an effective treatment for bipolar disorder. It can provide support, education, and guidance to people with bipolar disorder and their families. Some psychotherapy treatments used to treat bipolar disorder include:

- Cognitive behavioral therapy (CBT)
- Family-focused therapy
- Interpersonal and social rhythm therapy
- Psychoeducation

Visit the NIMH Psychotherapies webpage to learn about the various types of psychotherapies.

REFERENCES/RESOURCES

www.nimh.nih.gov

www.nami.org

BOOKS:

His Bright Light, Danielle Steel

Books by Kay Redfield Jamison

Darkness Falls Fast

An Unquite Mind

Touched With Fire:
Manic-Depressive Illness
and the Artistic Temperament

NATIONAL SUICIDE PREVENTION LIFELINE
1-800-273-(TALK)8255
TTY: 1-800-799-4TTY (4889)

VETERANS CRISIS LINE
1-877-958-0126

About the Author

Michelle earned a B.S. in Elementary Education from Penn State University and later earned her Structural Welding Certificate from the Central PA Institute of Science and Technology. where She lives in the beautiful Victorian town of Bellefonte, PA with her three cats, Cornelius, Stella and Magnus.

She enjoys doing traditional arts like sewing, quilting, and embroidery, but has had fun over the years doing more unusual projects like creating bowling shirts and a hand-sequened Elvis jumpsuit for stuffed animals. She also likes to do welded steel wall art, a nd can always be found working on some project around the house. She still likes to white water slalom kayak, watch the stars and dreams of visiting Mykonos, Greece.

She has written three children's books and is working on a novel, all of which she hopes to publish in the future.

Of all the things she has done in her life she most cherishes the time she has spent with her children and she is happiest being known as "mom".

46489623R00092

Made in the USA
Middletown, DE
28 May 2019